Copyright Information.

No part of this book may be reproduced or kept
in any form of retrieval system,
electronic or otherwise.
Save that the original purchaser only,
may make physical photocopies
of individual designs for there own personal use.

©Peter Clark All rights Reserved

Coloring Minds

60 Mandala Images to Relax the Mind

Volume 1

Pocket Edition

By Peter Clark

Copyright © 2015 by Peter Clark.

Published by Red Berry Quiz Books

Printed by CreateSpace

Available from Amazon.com,
CreateSpace.com,
and other retail outlets

Message from the author

Thank you for buying this colouring book, which will bring hours of relaxing pleasure.

Colouring can be done anywhere, at anytime and
requires no electricity, internet connections or any device.
In the car, on the beach, in the park, in your lunch break in fact anywhere.

Coloured pencils, marker pens or paints are all that is required, for you to lose yourself in your art.
For best results place a piece of paper under the page being colored, to prevent bleed through of inks and paints or denting if using pencils.

All designs in this book are copyright, however you are allowed to
photocopy the designs for you to colour. This will keep your book in new condition and allow you to colour the designs over and over again in different colours.

Use your book anytime of the day. Choose a simple design if you have limited time or a more complex design when time permits.

Enjoy your colouring and look out for more of my colouring designs.

How to Use This Book

1. Choose your image, some can be completed in a few hours, others may take days to complete.
2. Use colored pens, markers, paints of your choice to color each image as you wish.
3. Place a sheet of paper under each image being colored to prevent denting of the page or color bleed through
4. Relax and enjoy yourself.

    Finished all the images? Look at other books from http://www.redberryquizbooks.com/color

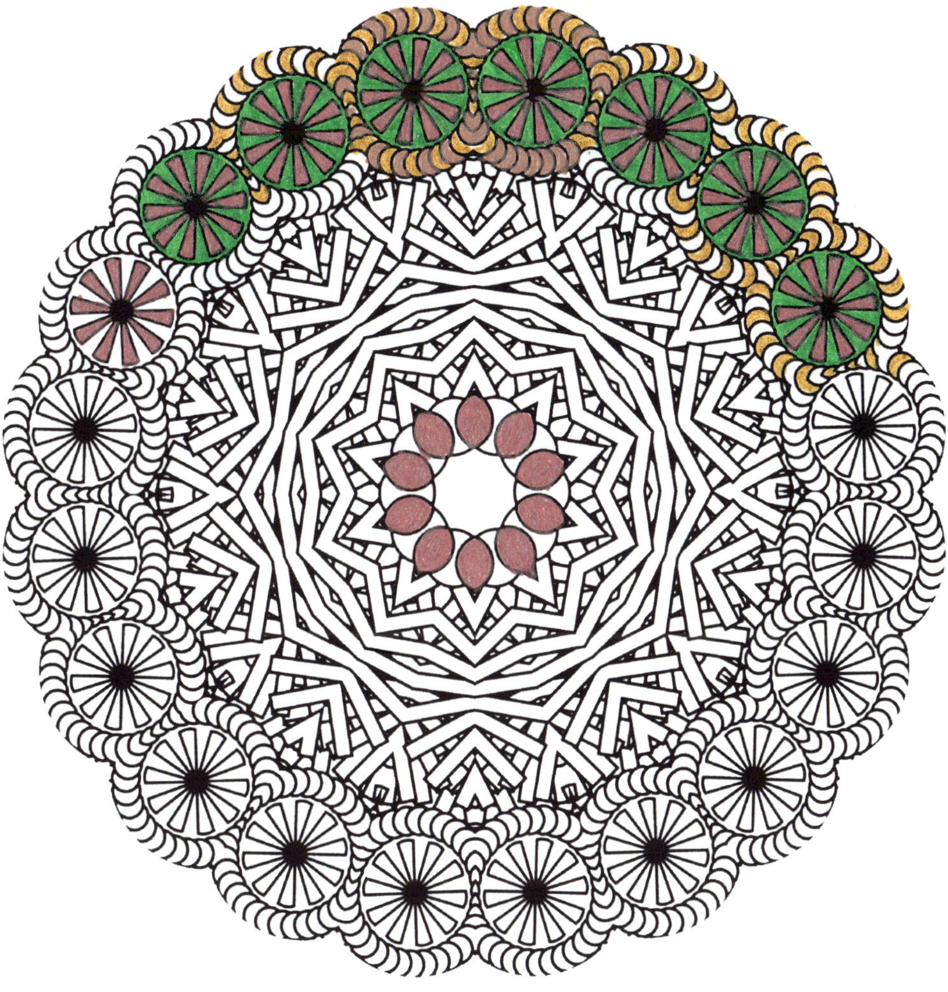

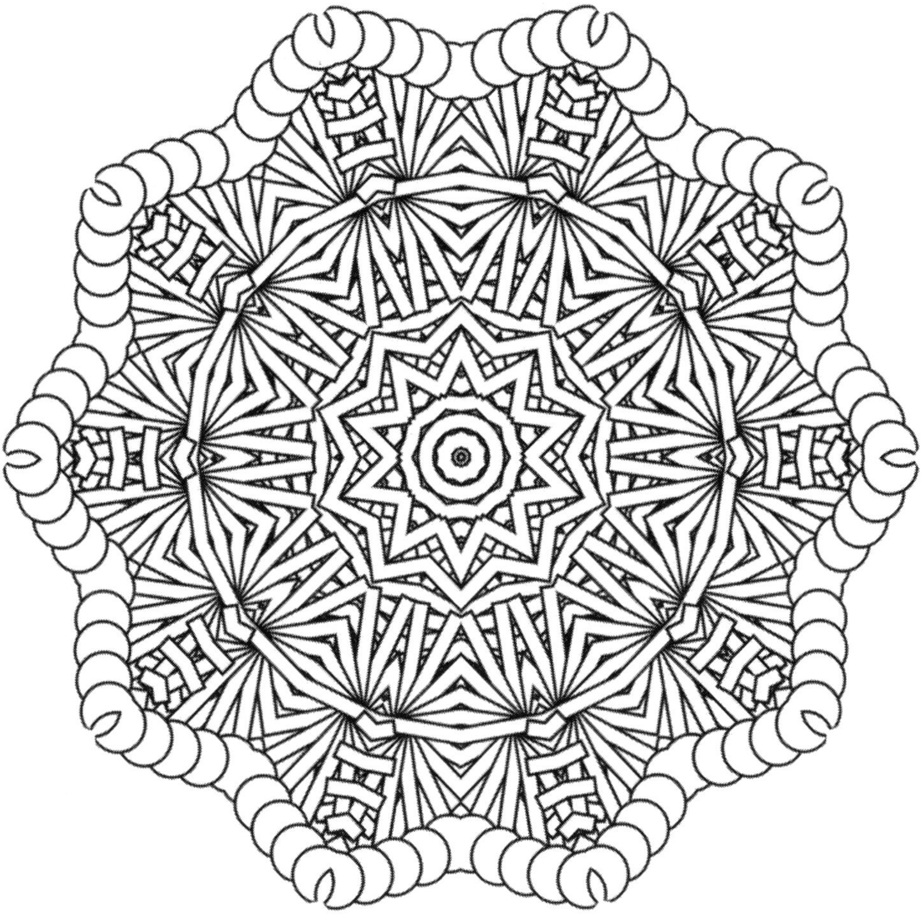

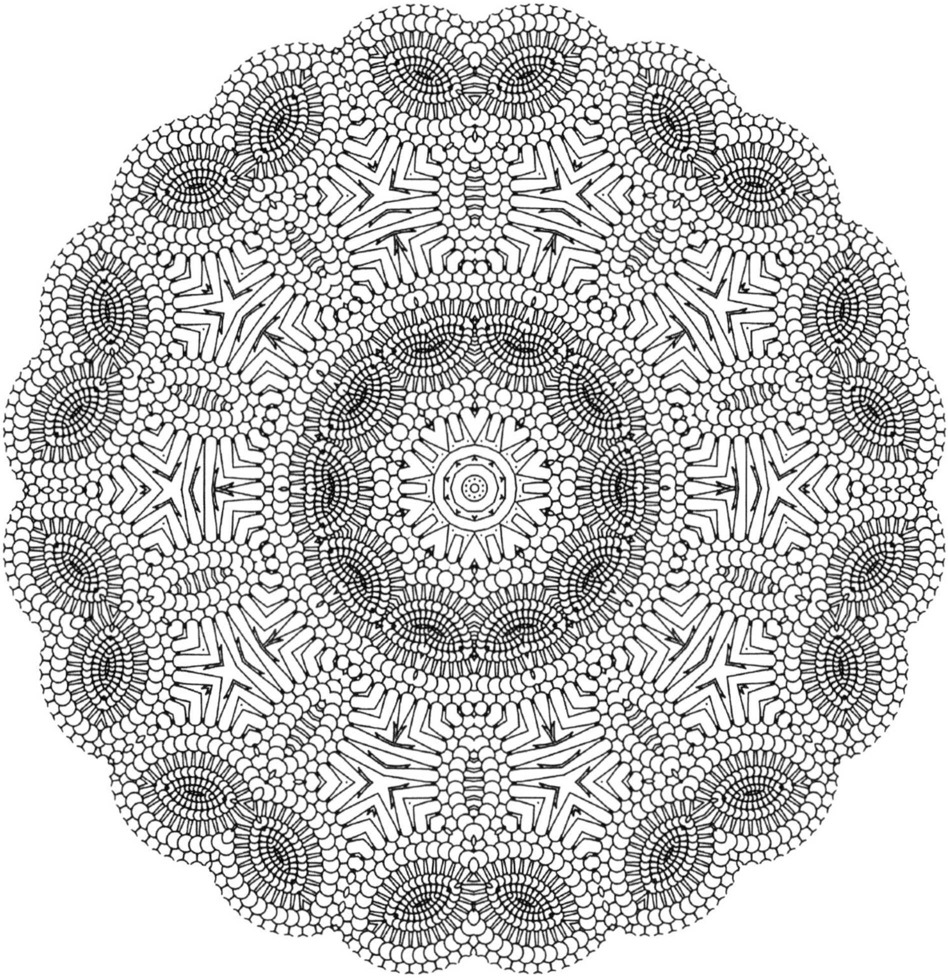

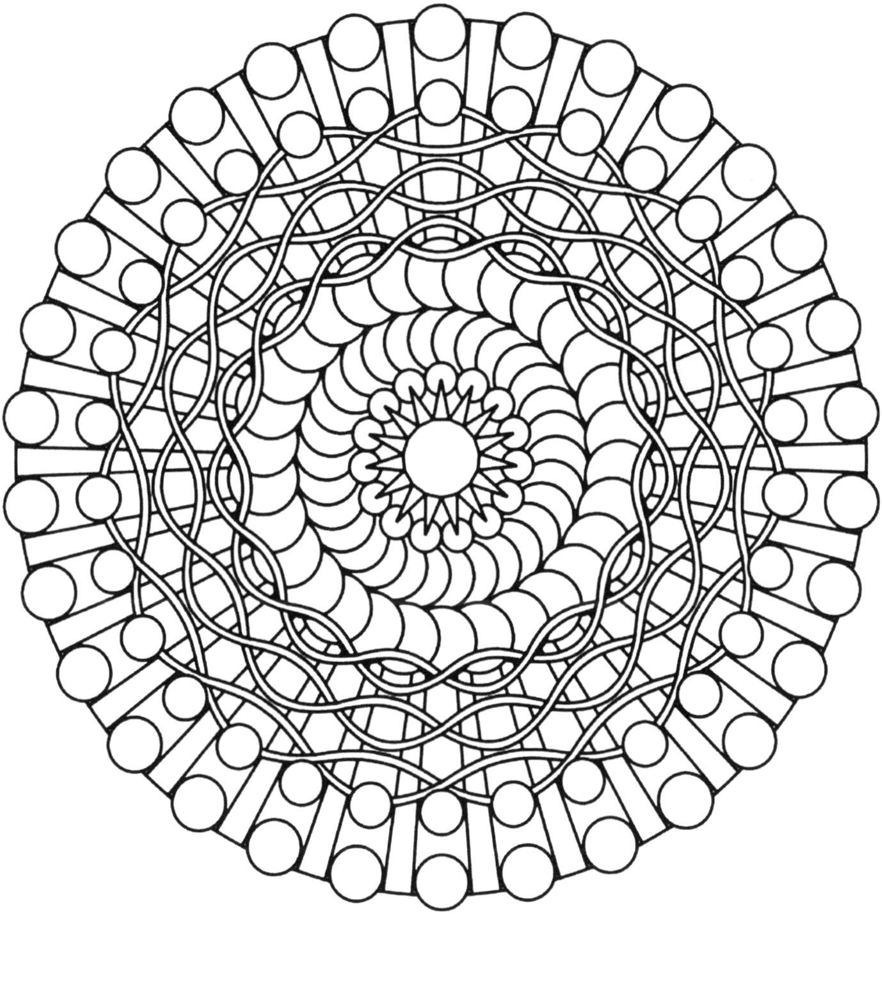

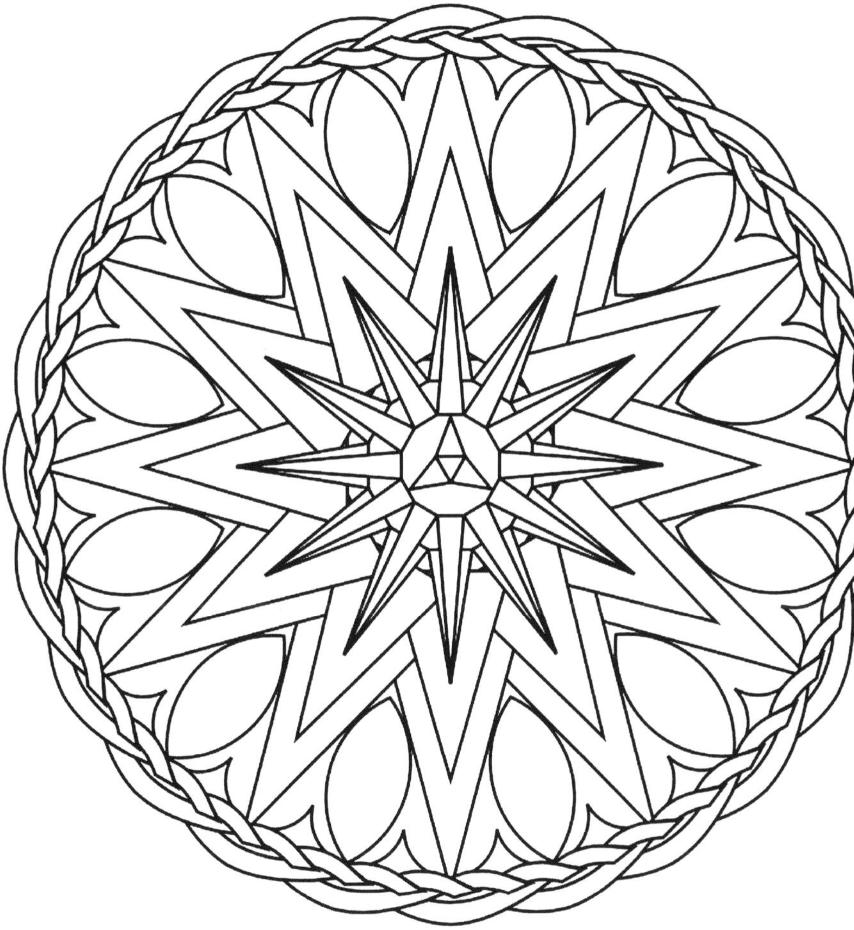

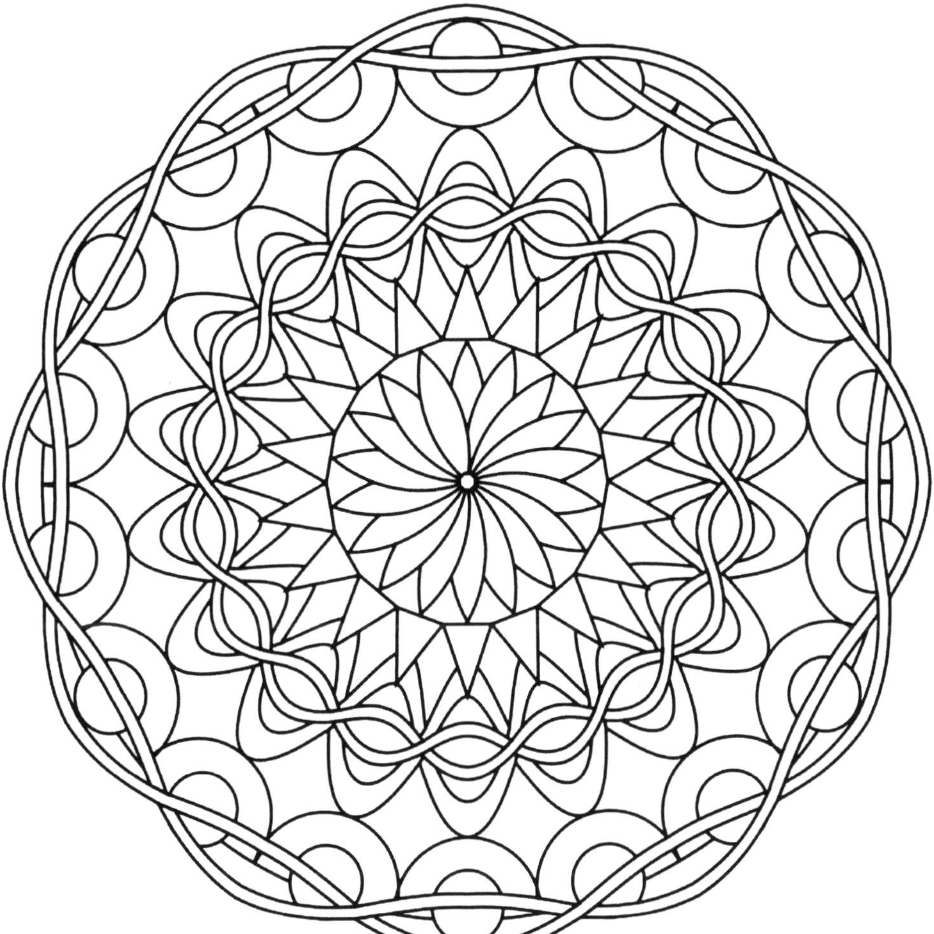

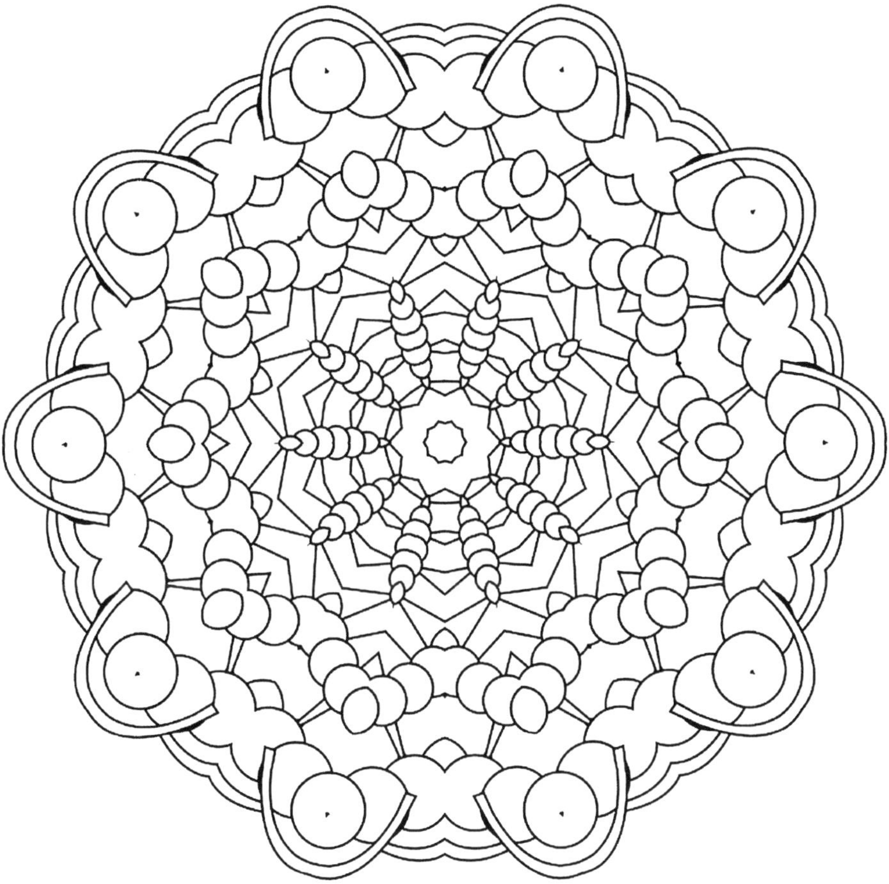

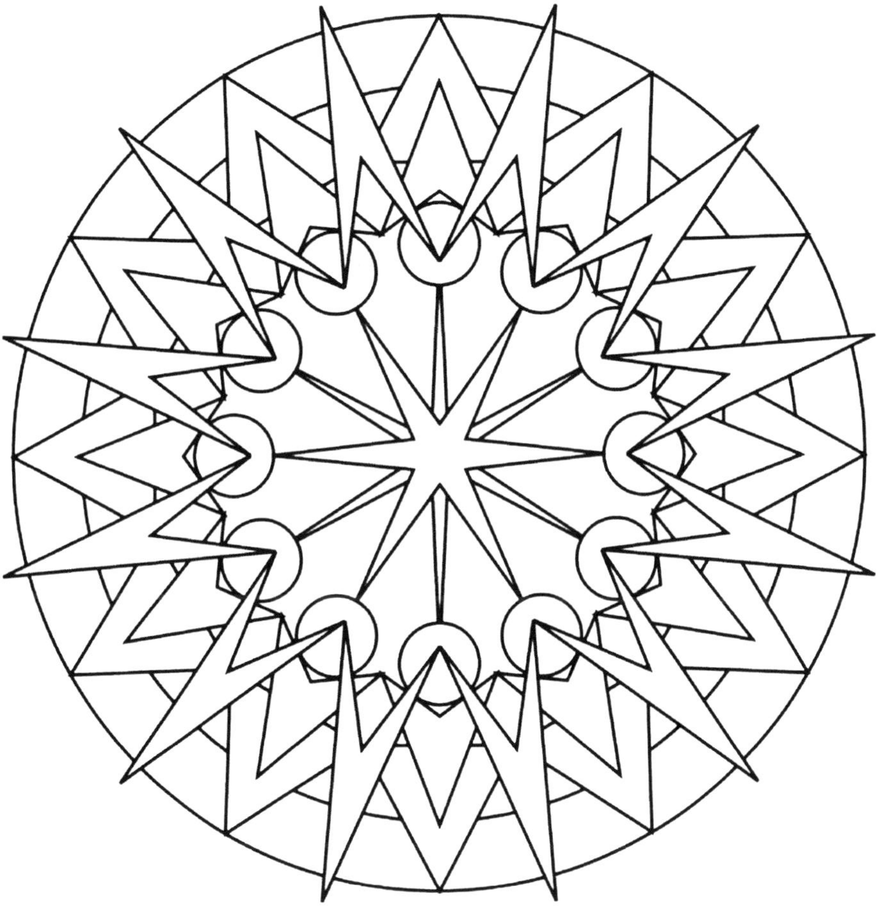

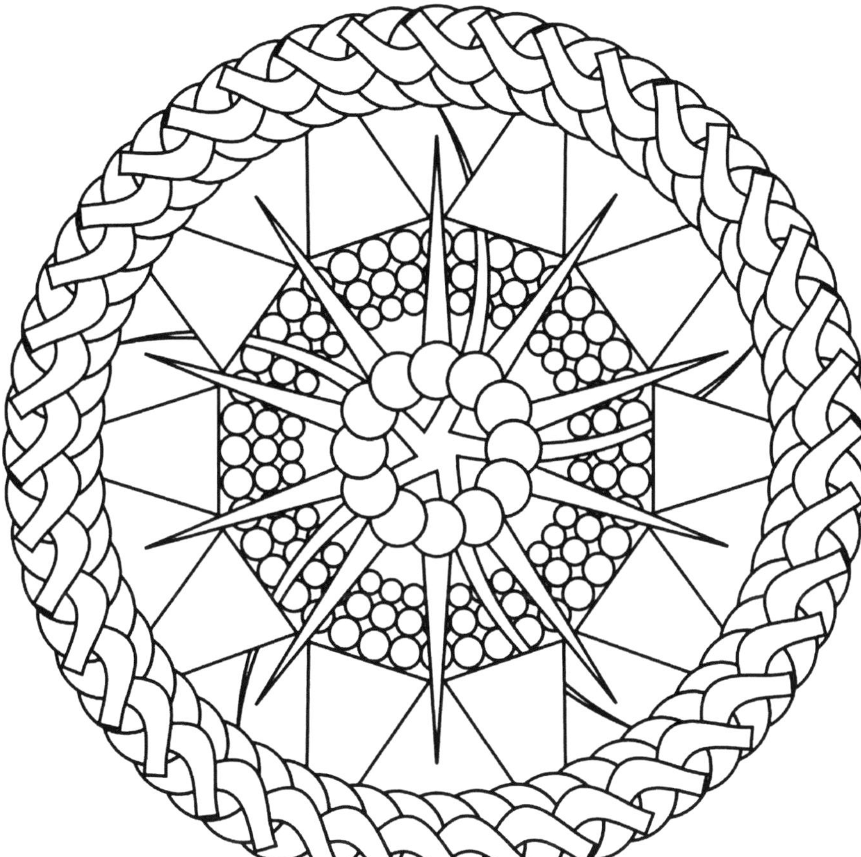

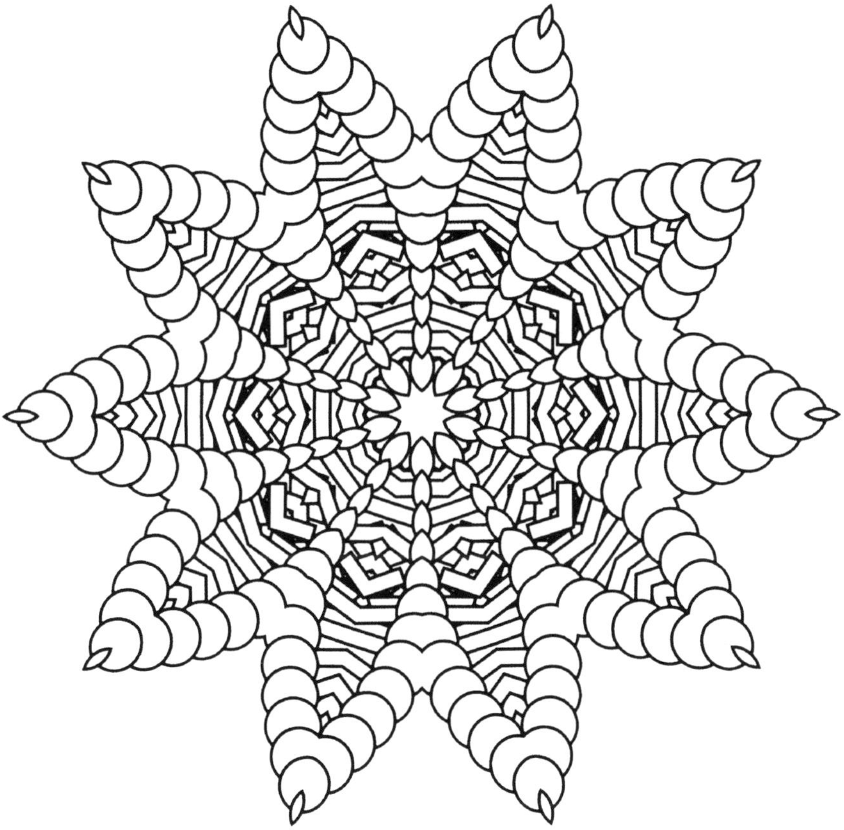

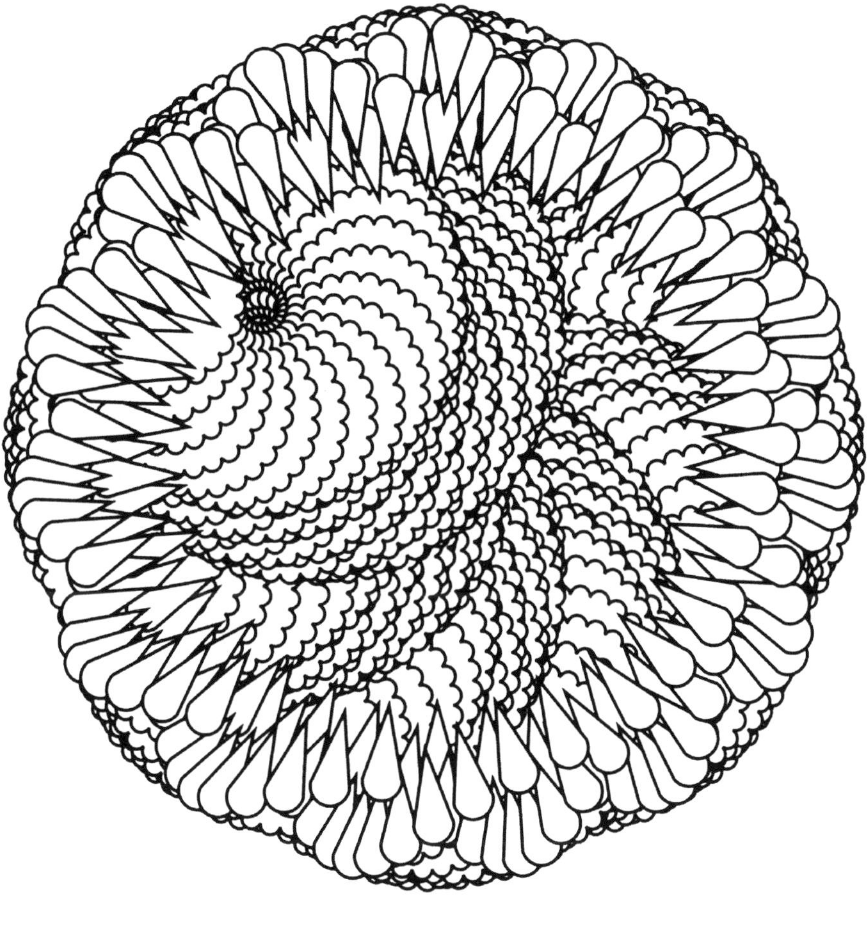

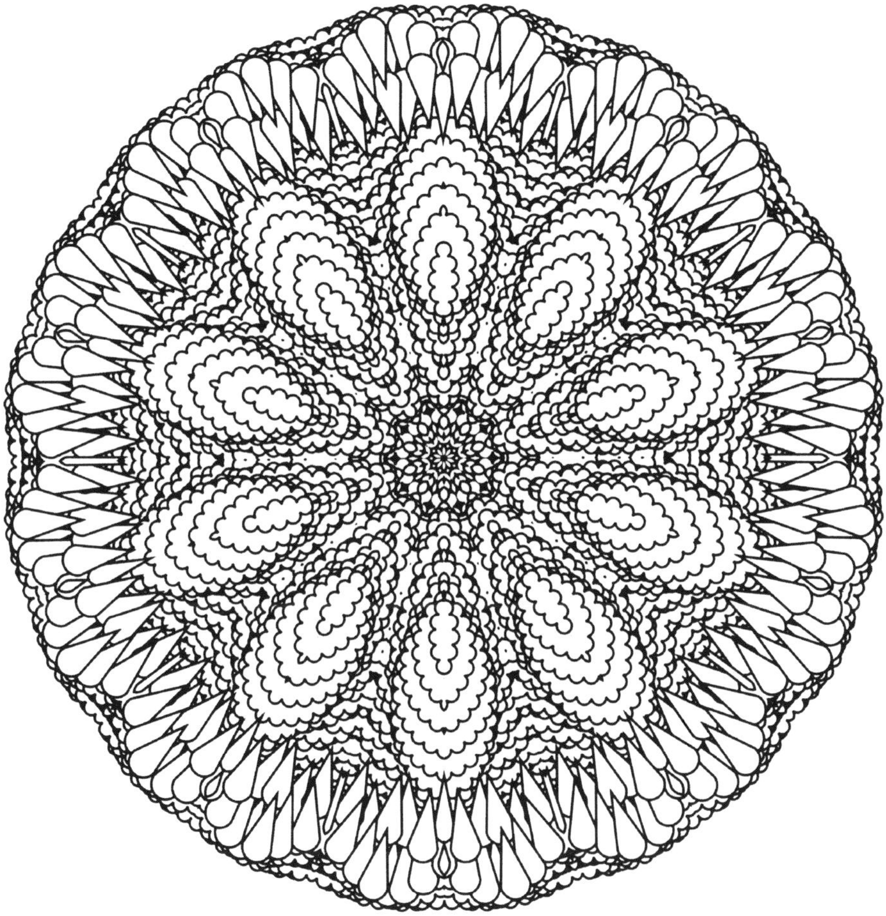

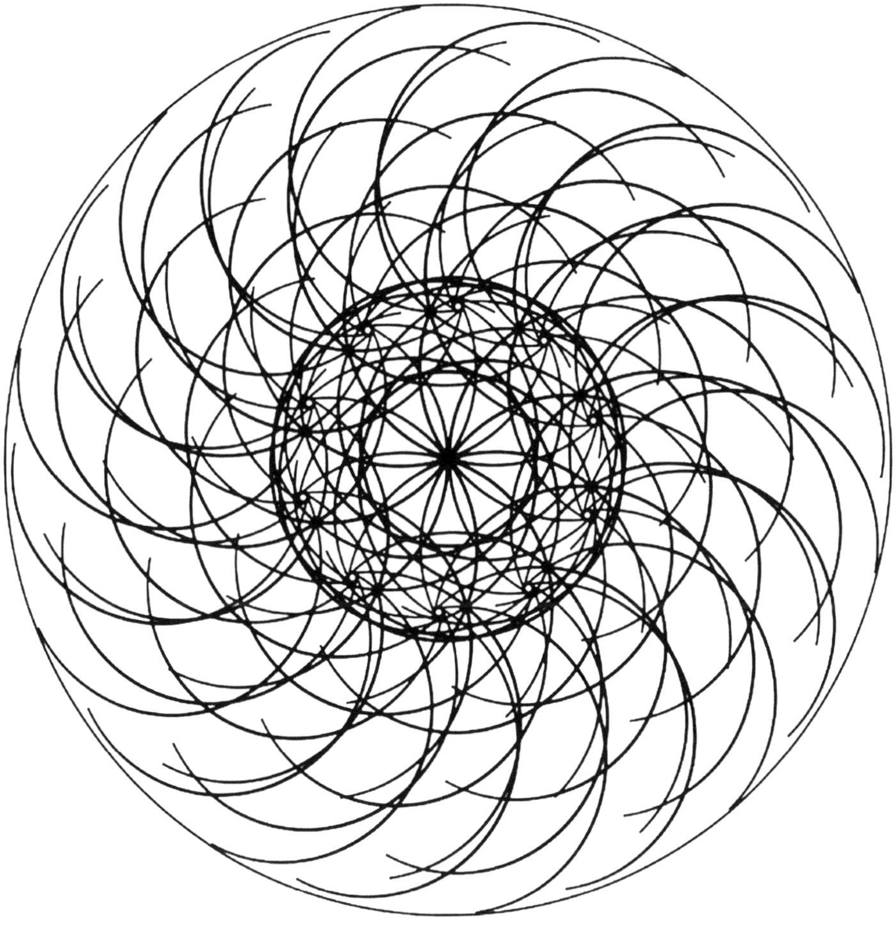

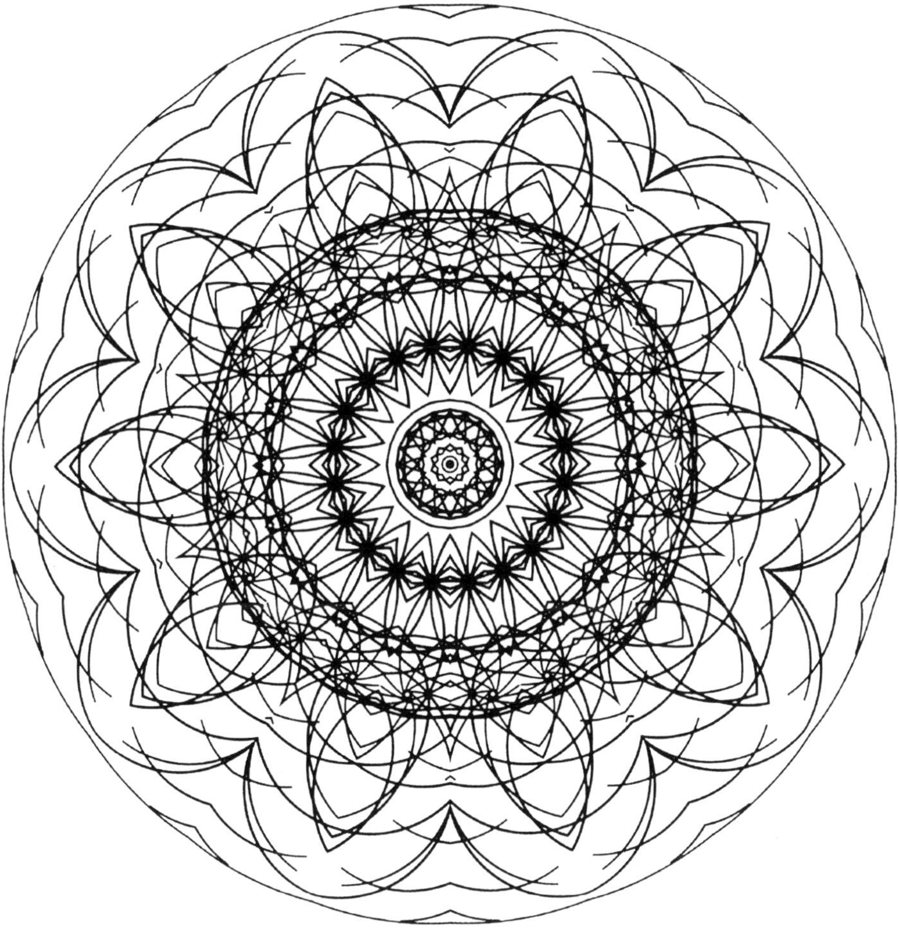

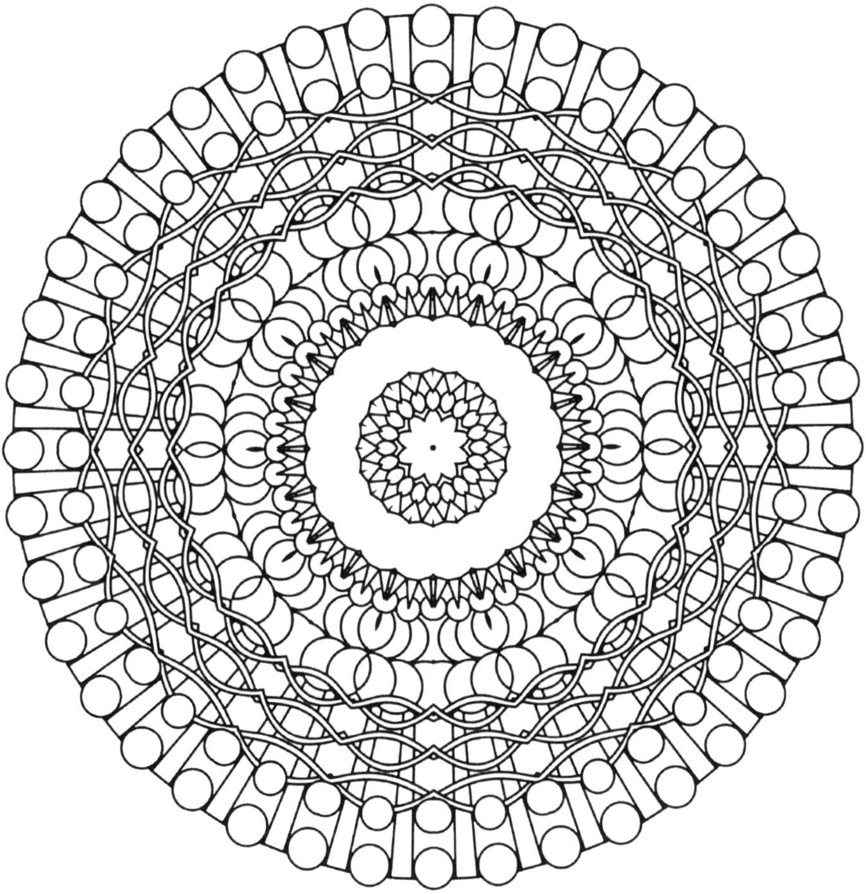

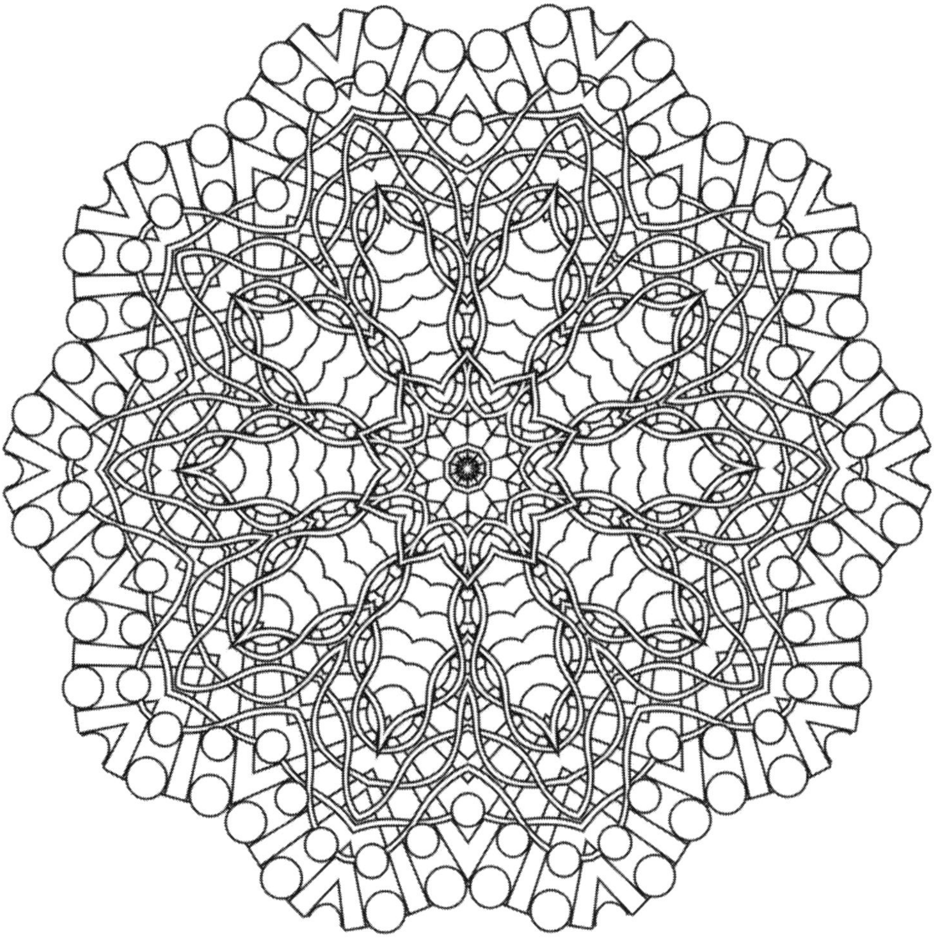

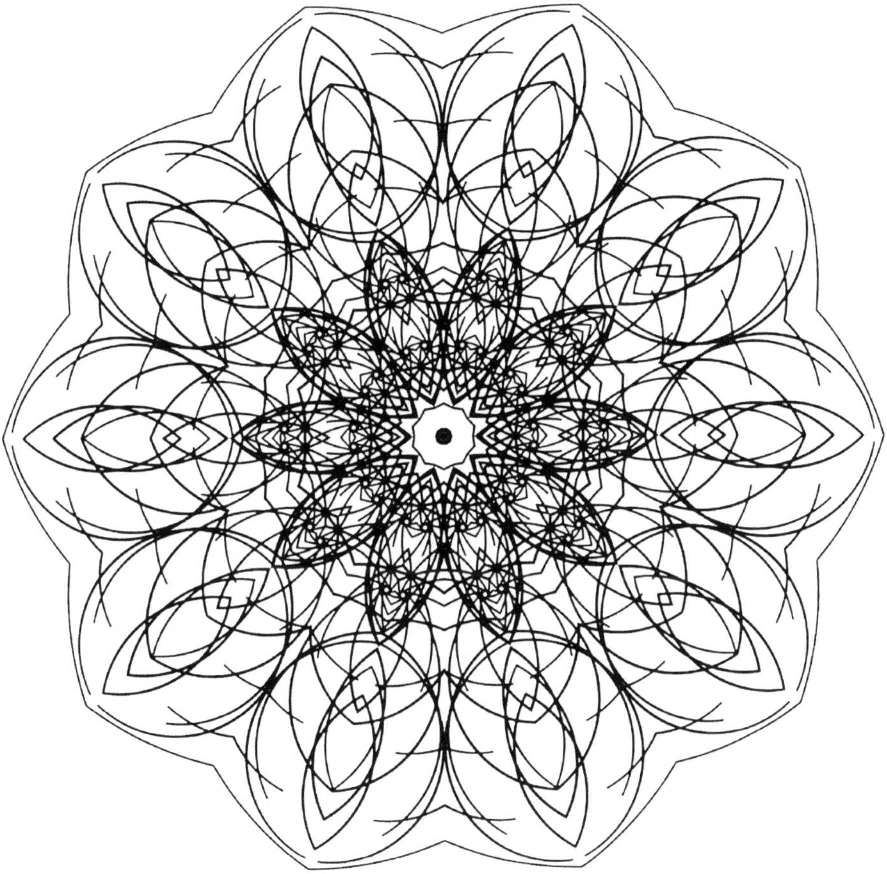

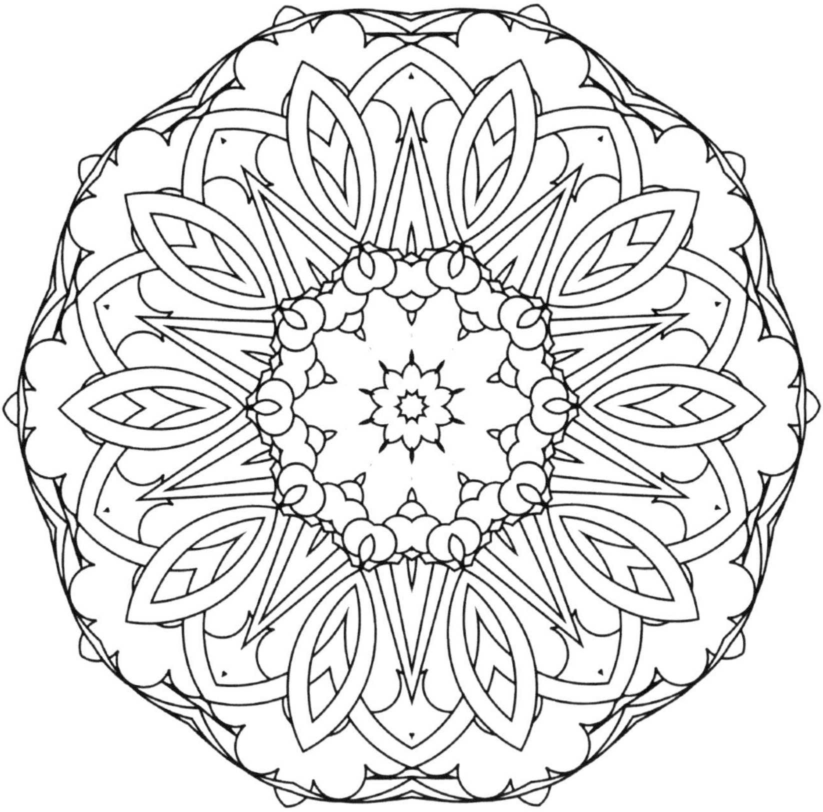

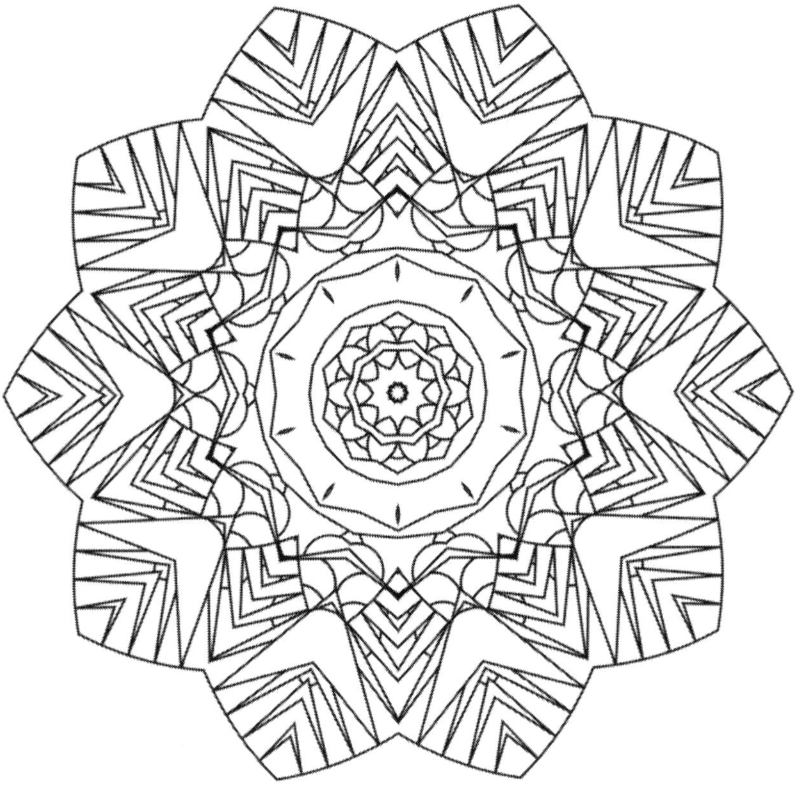

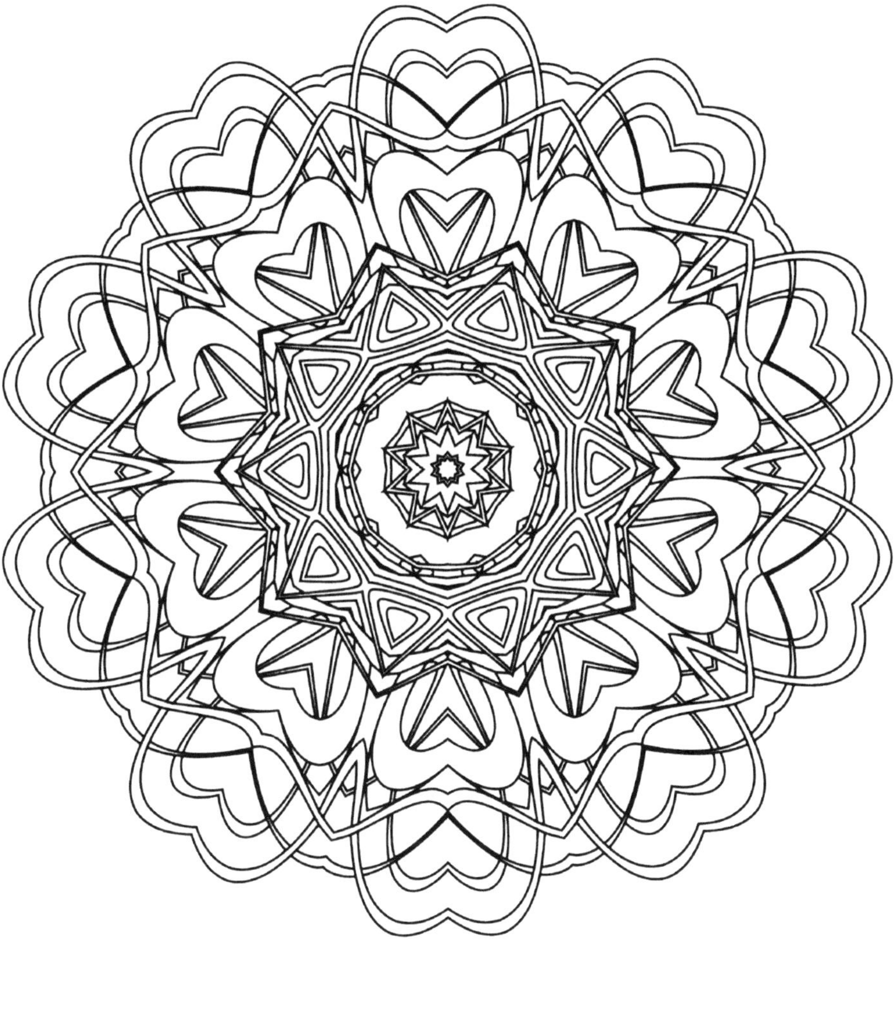

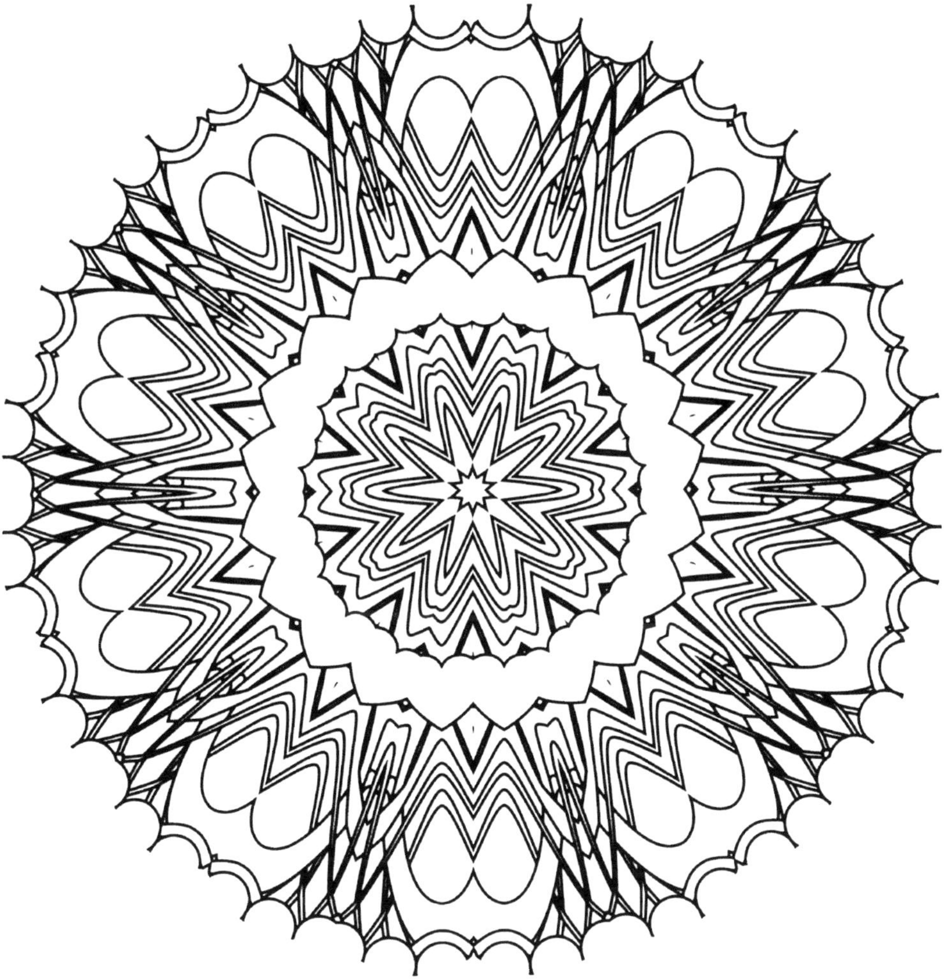

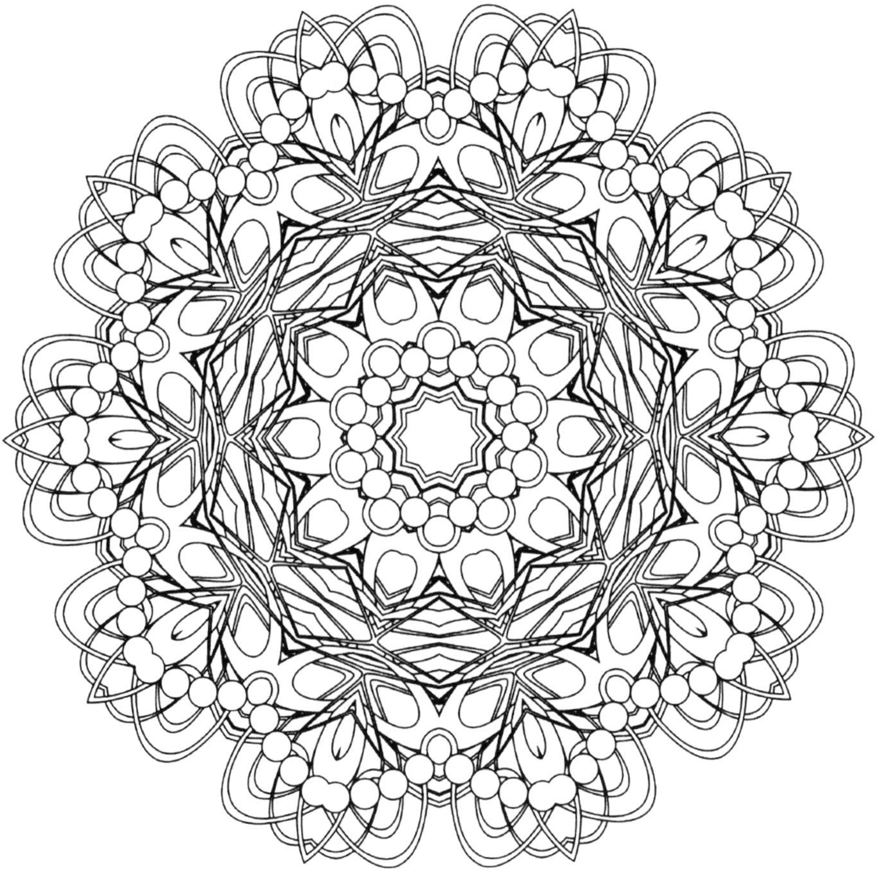

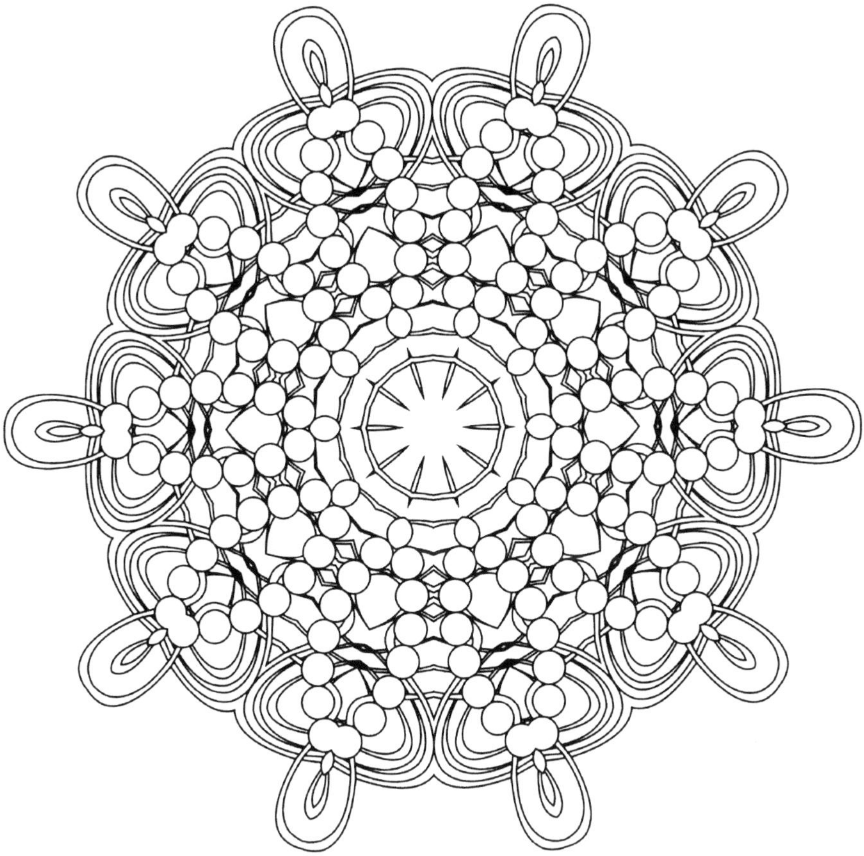

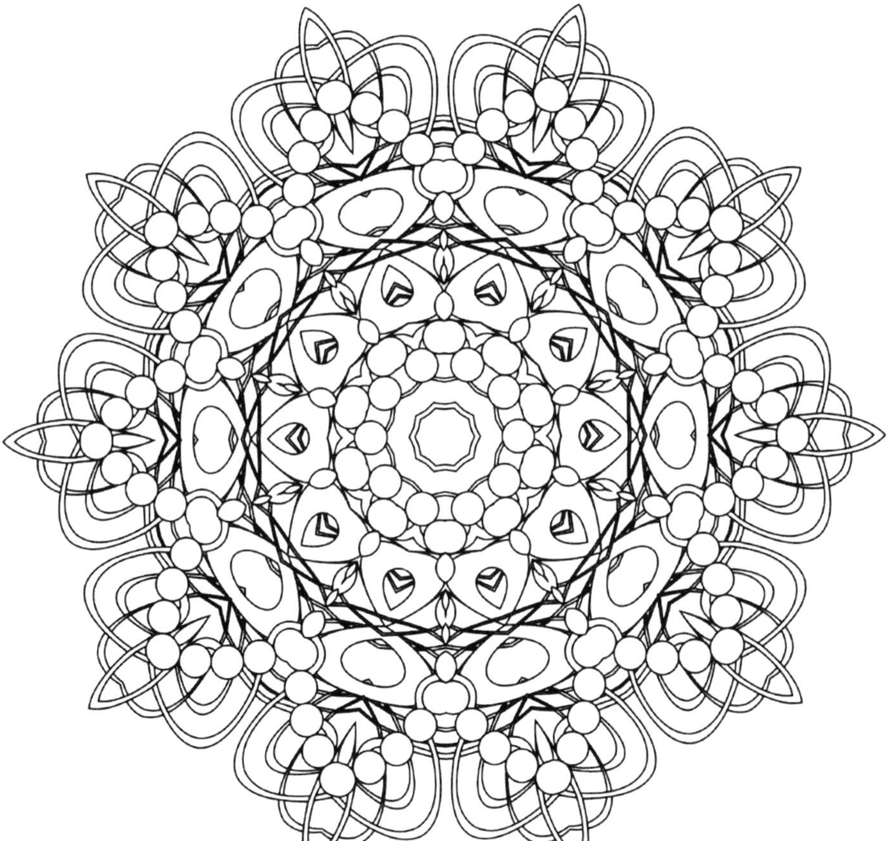

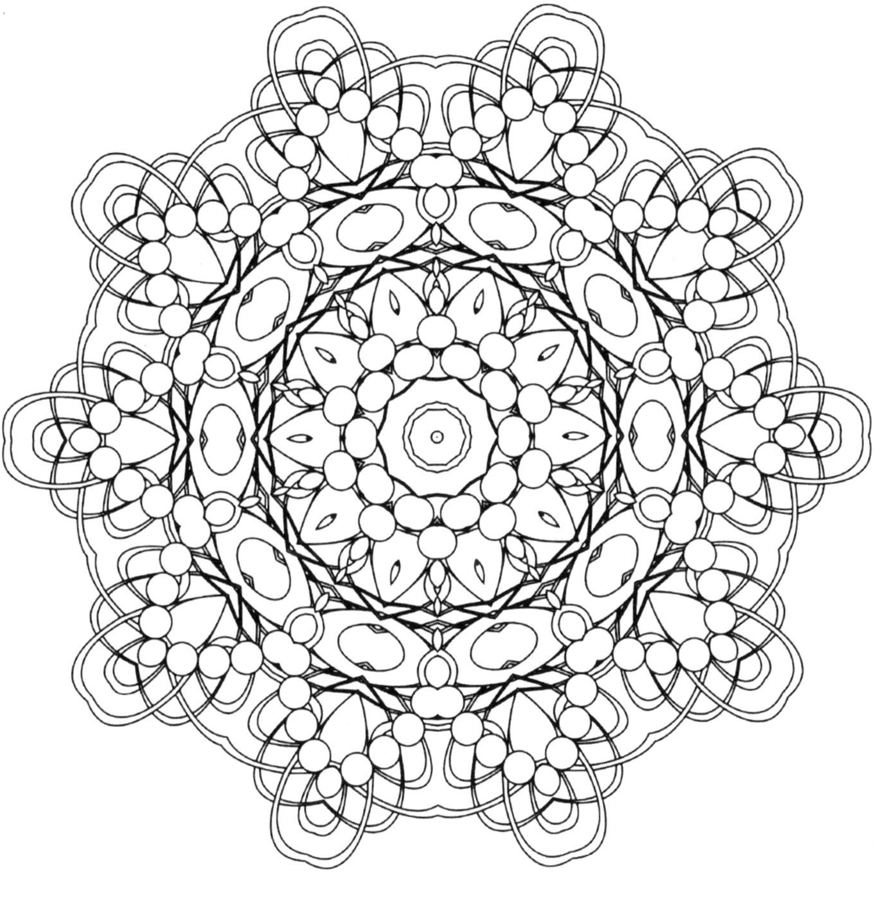

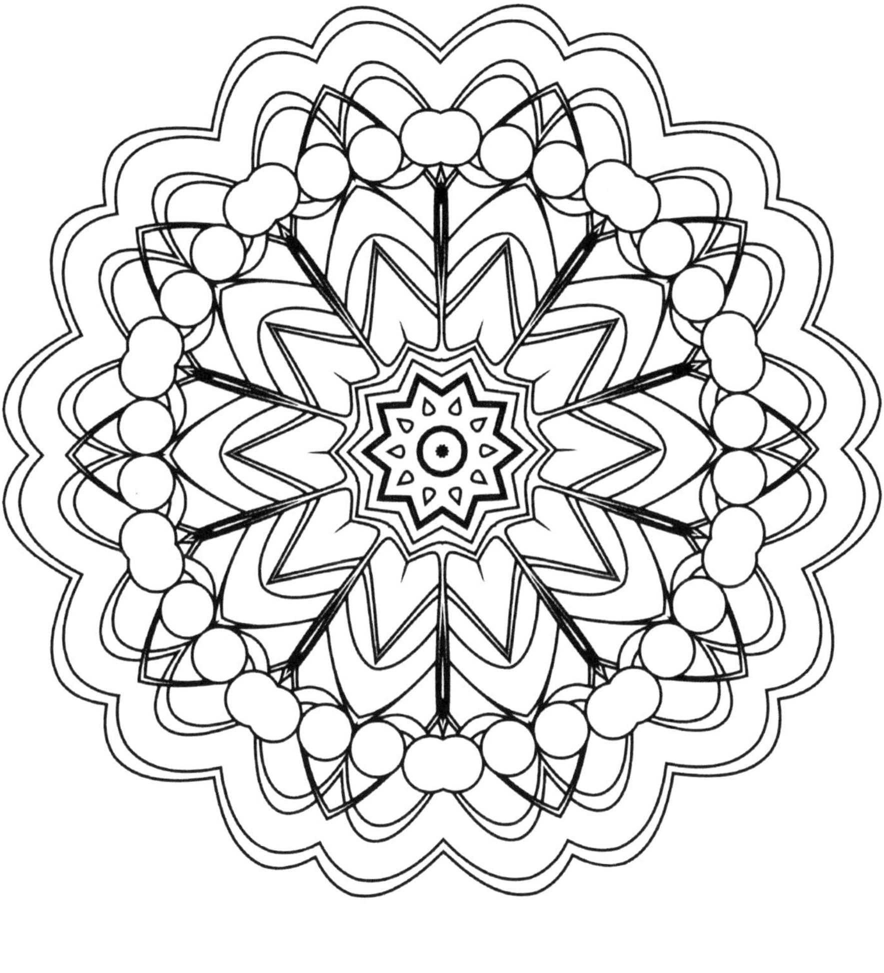

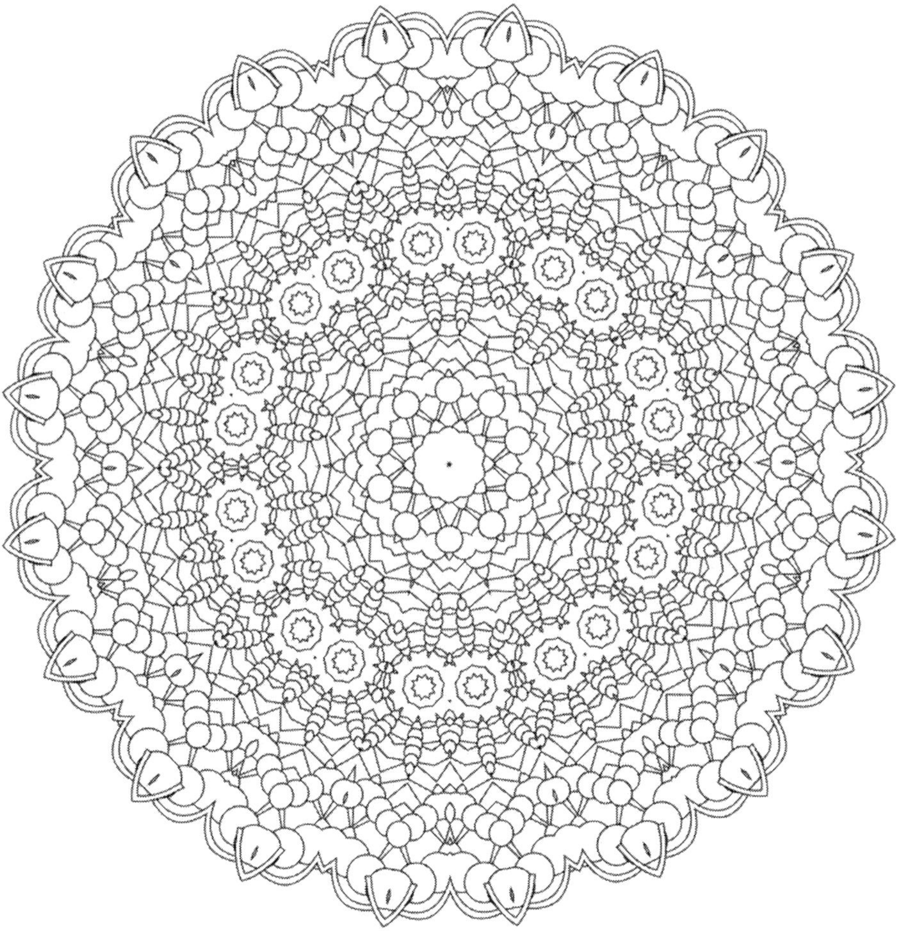

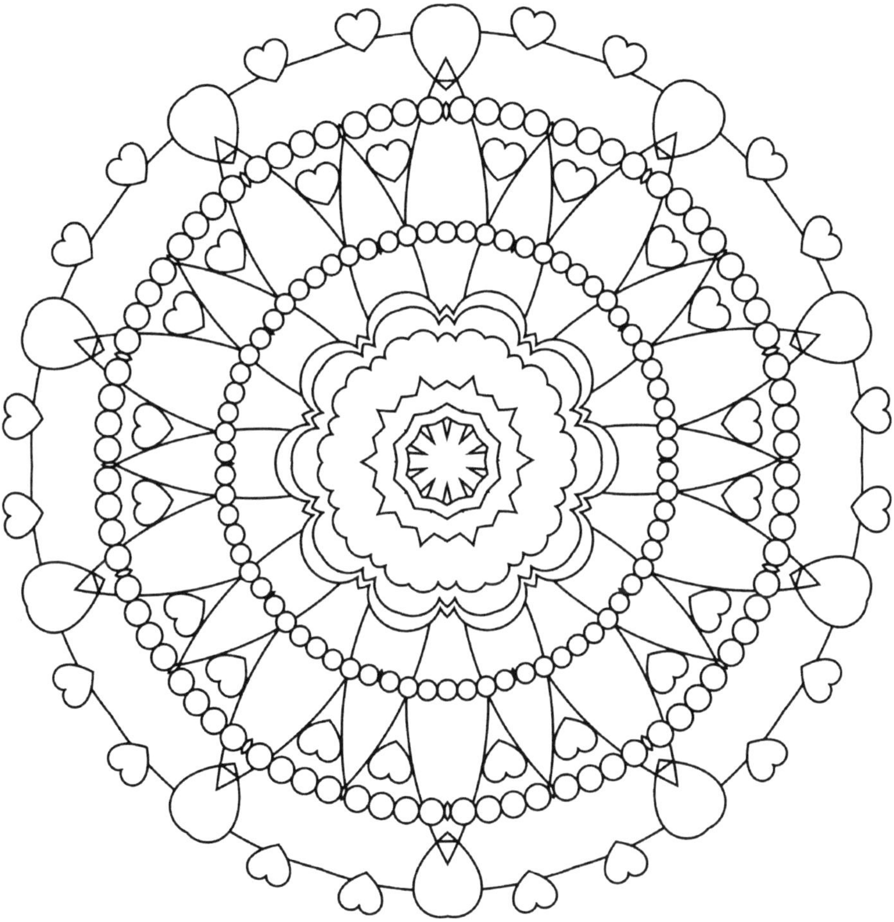

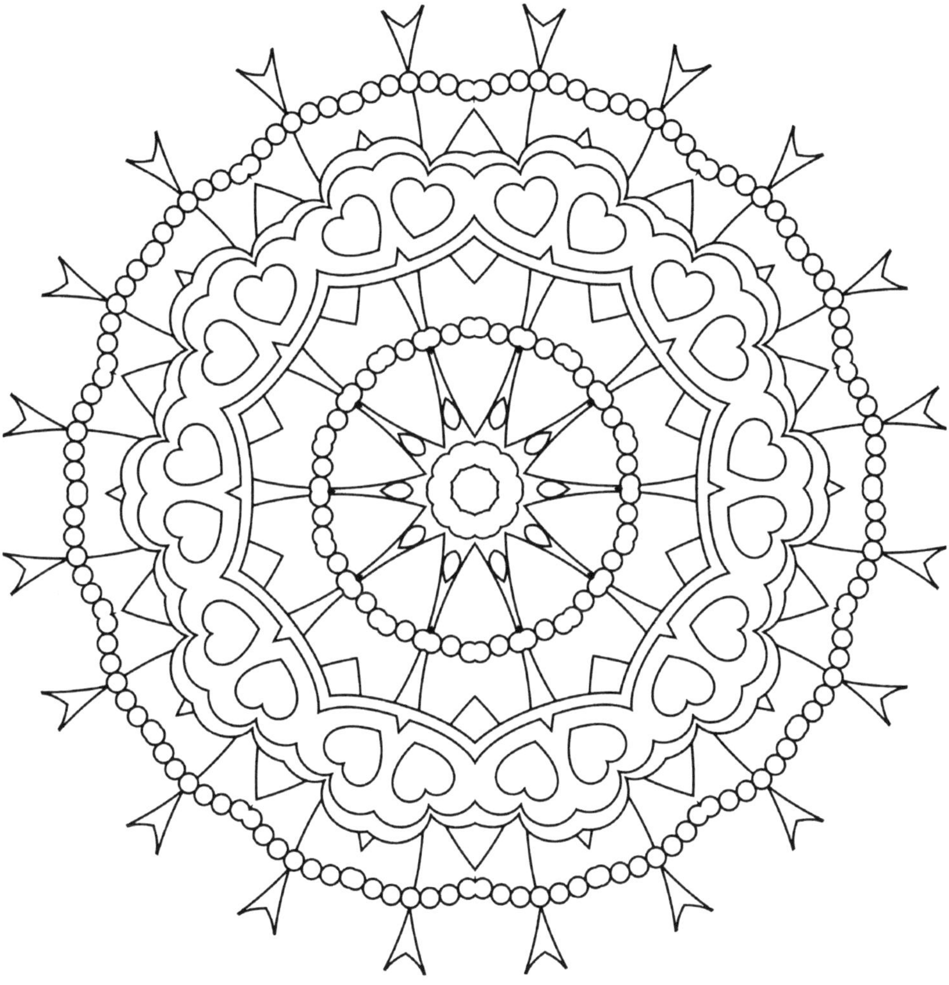

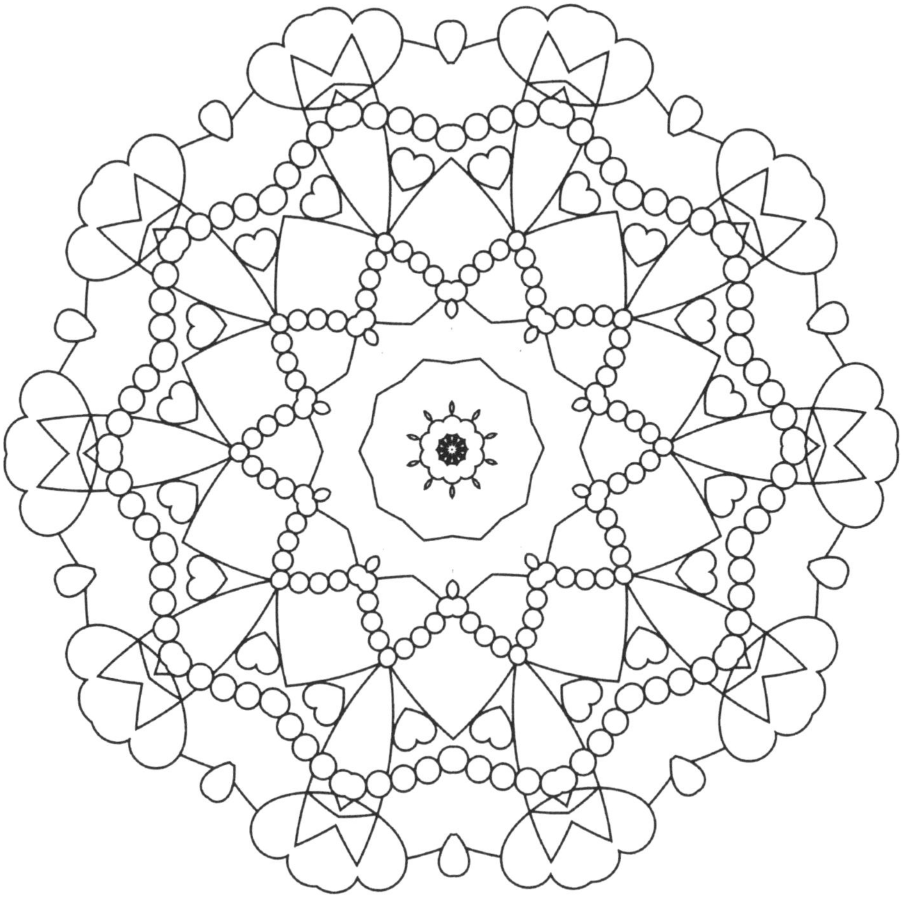

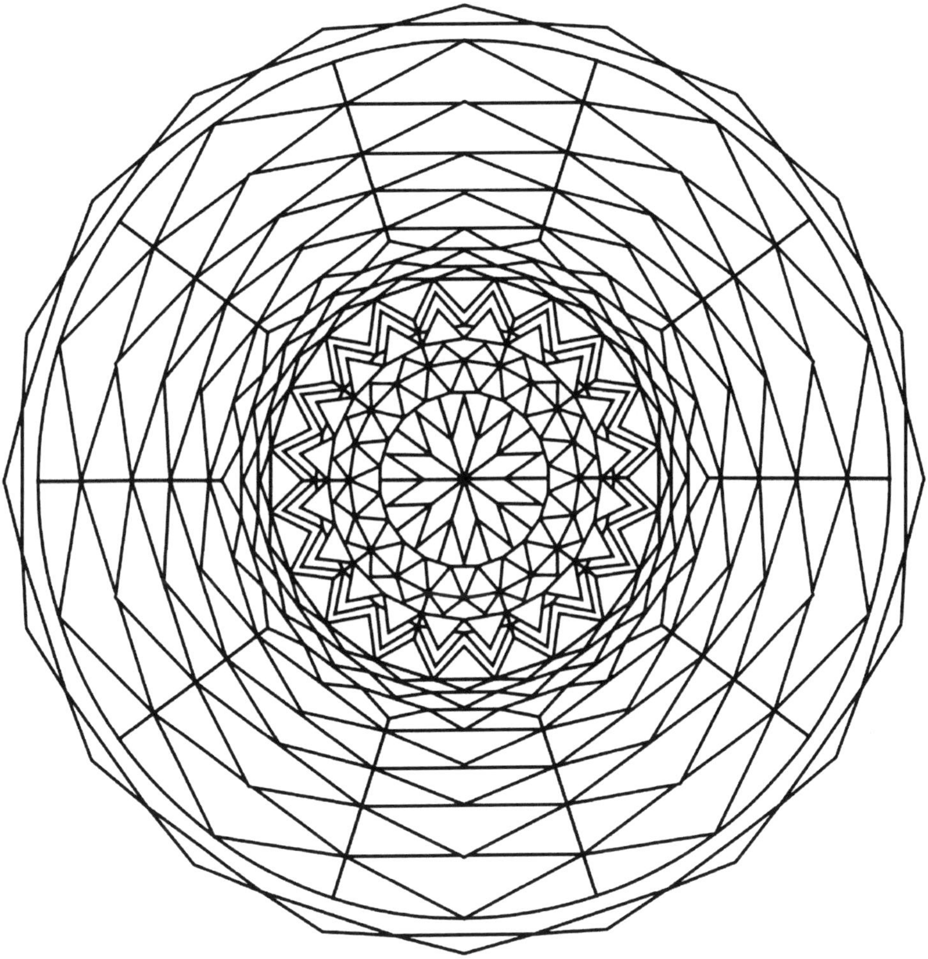

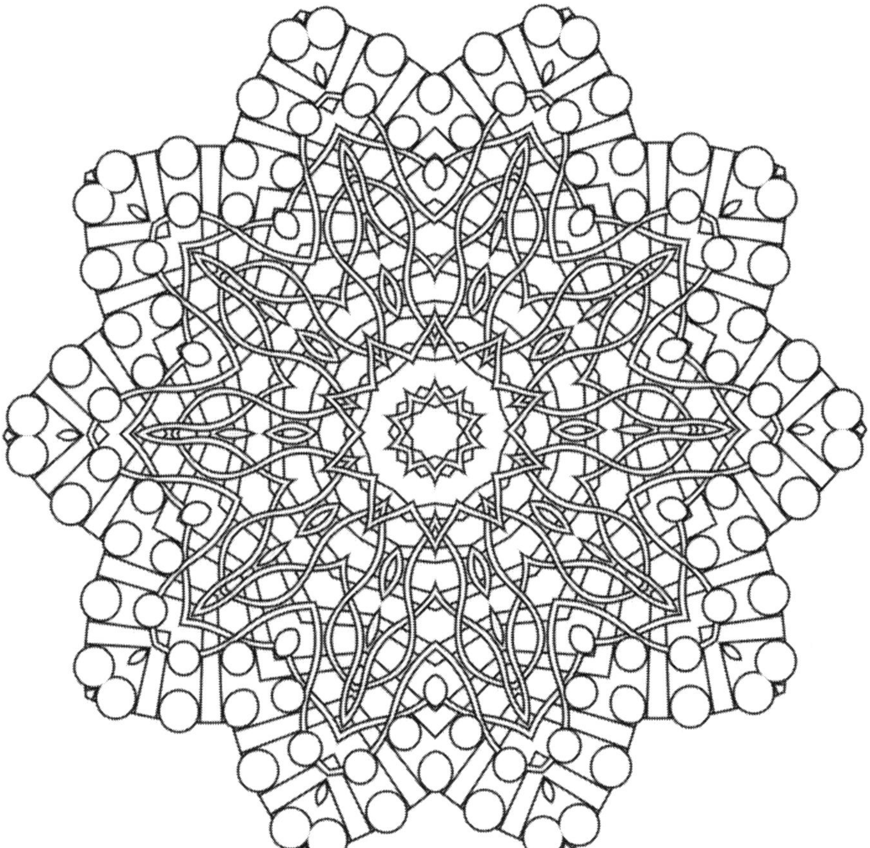

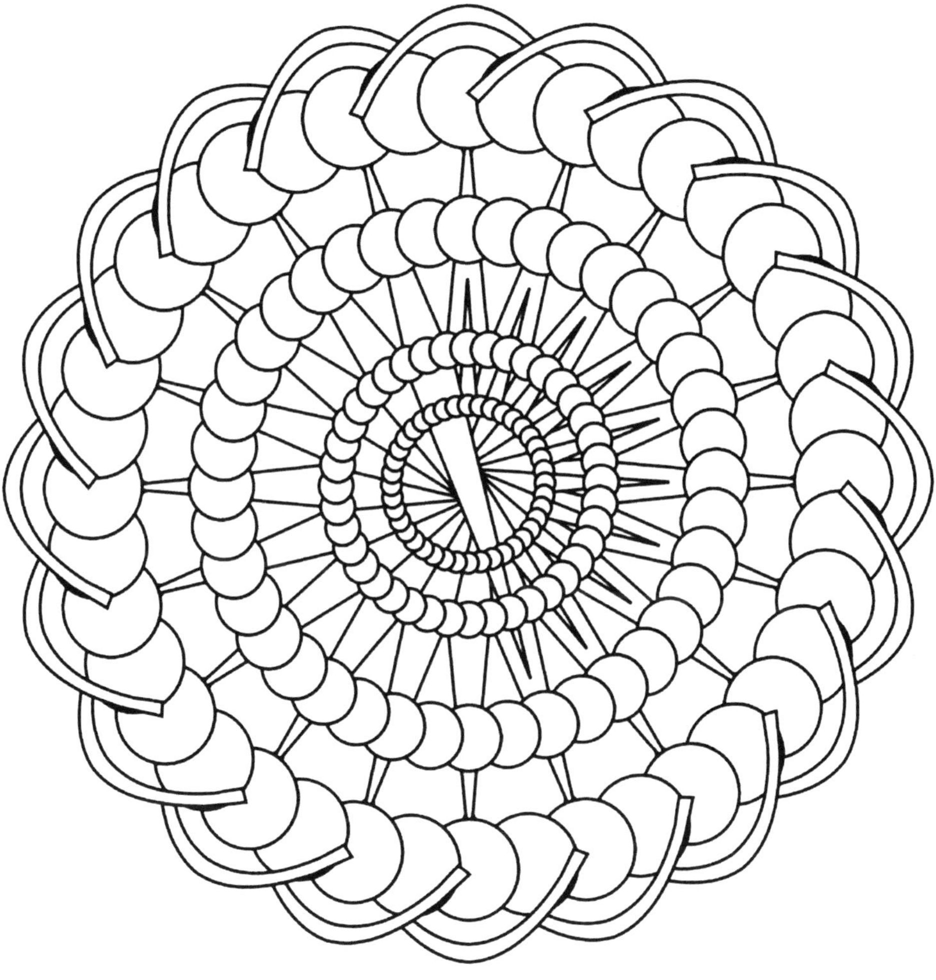

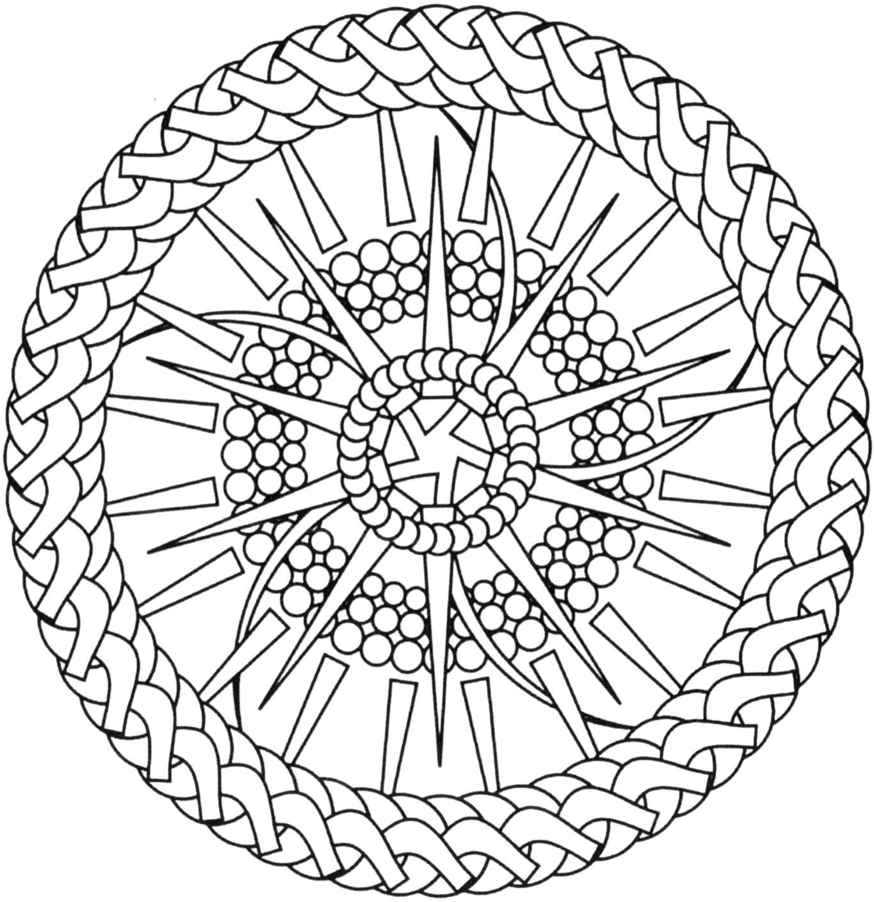

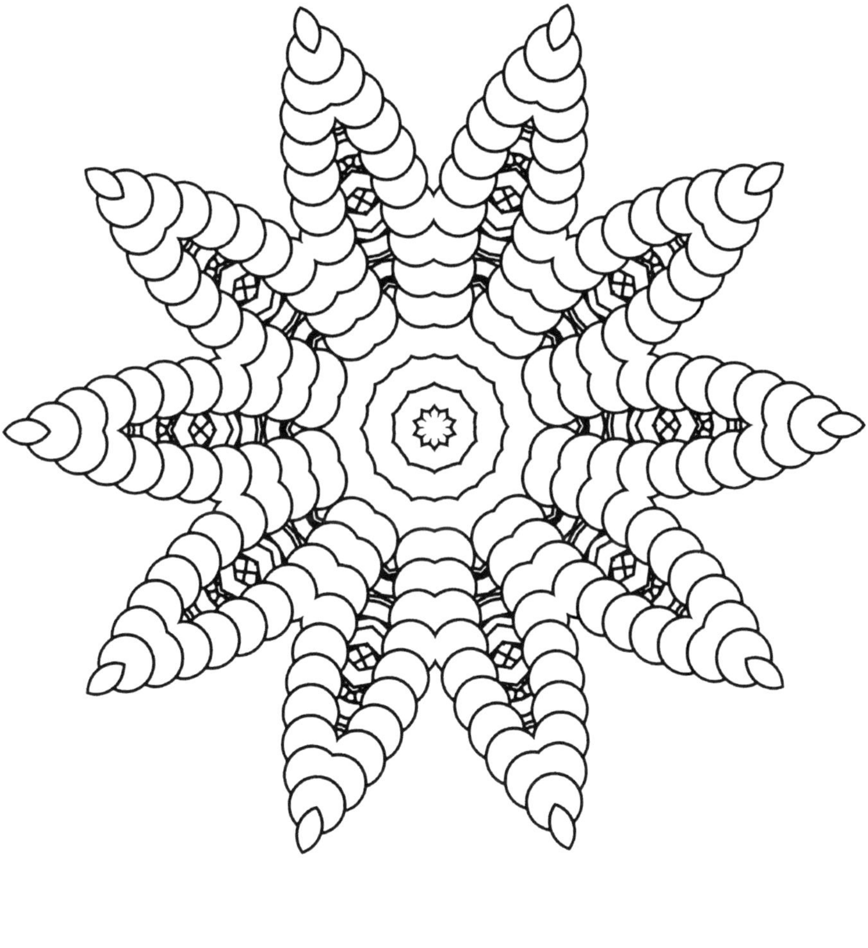

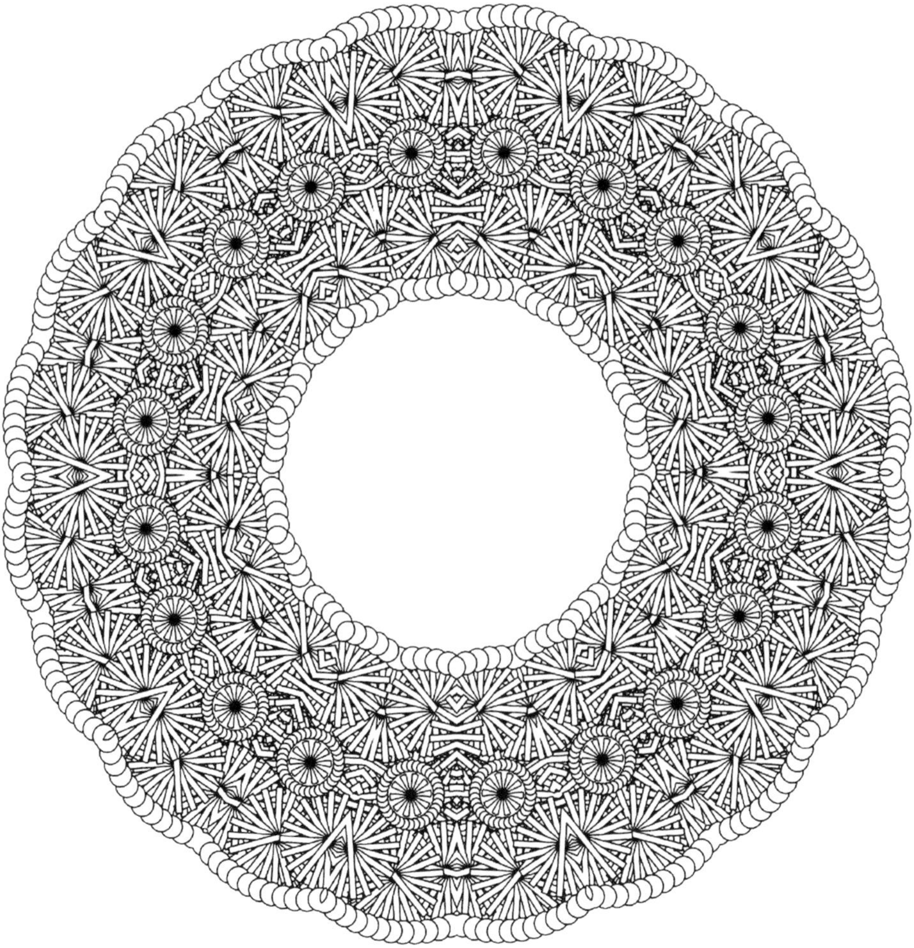

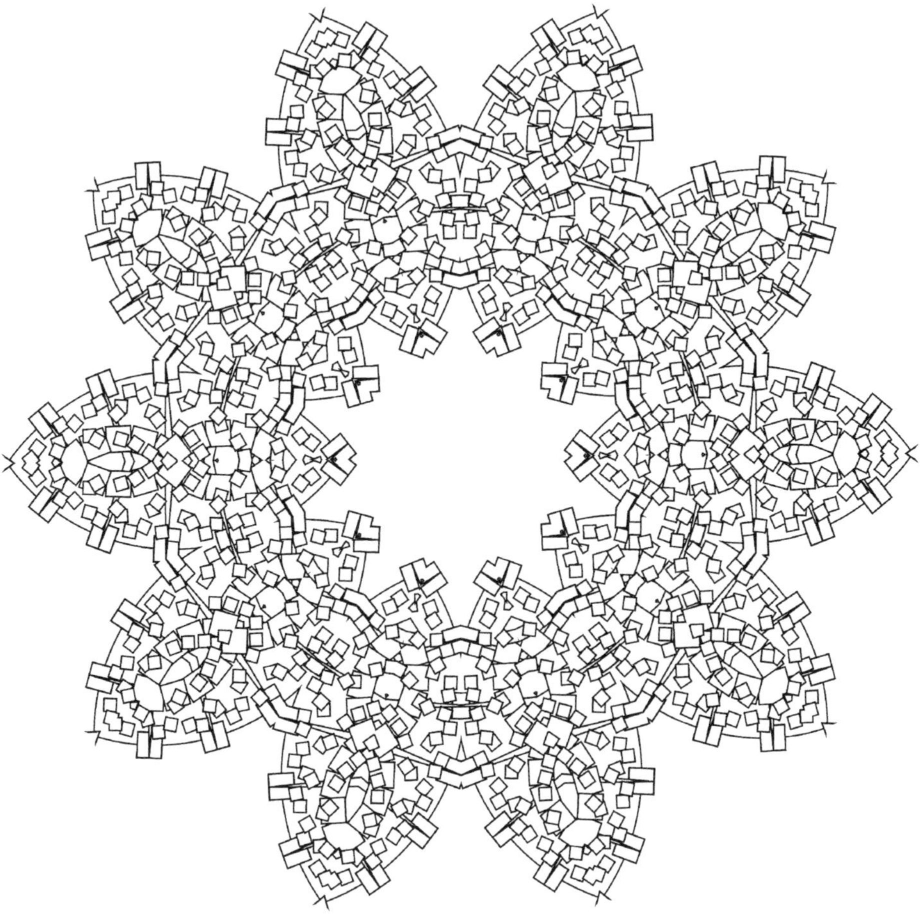

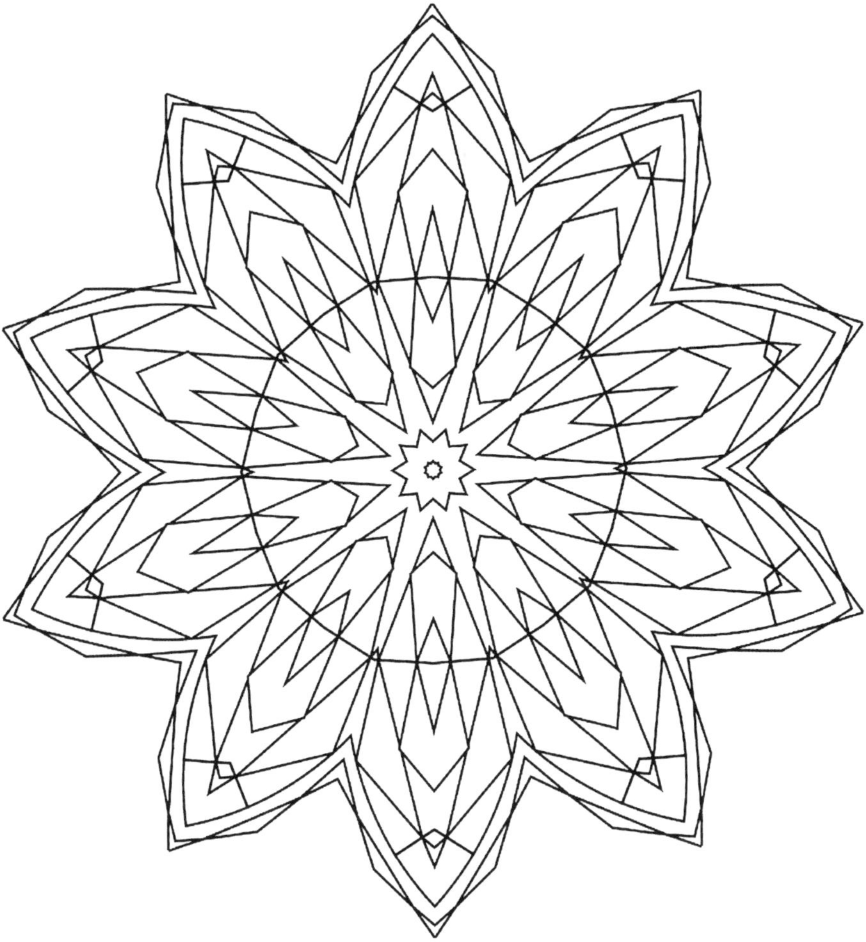

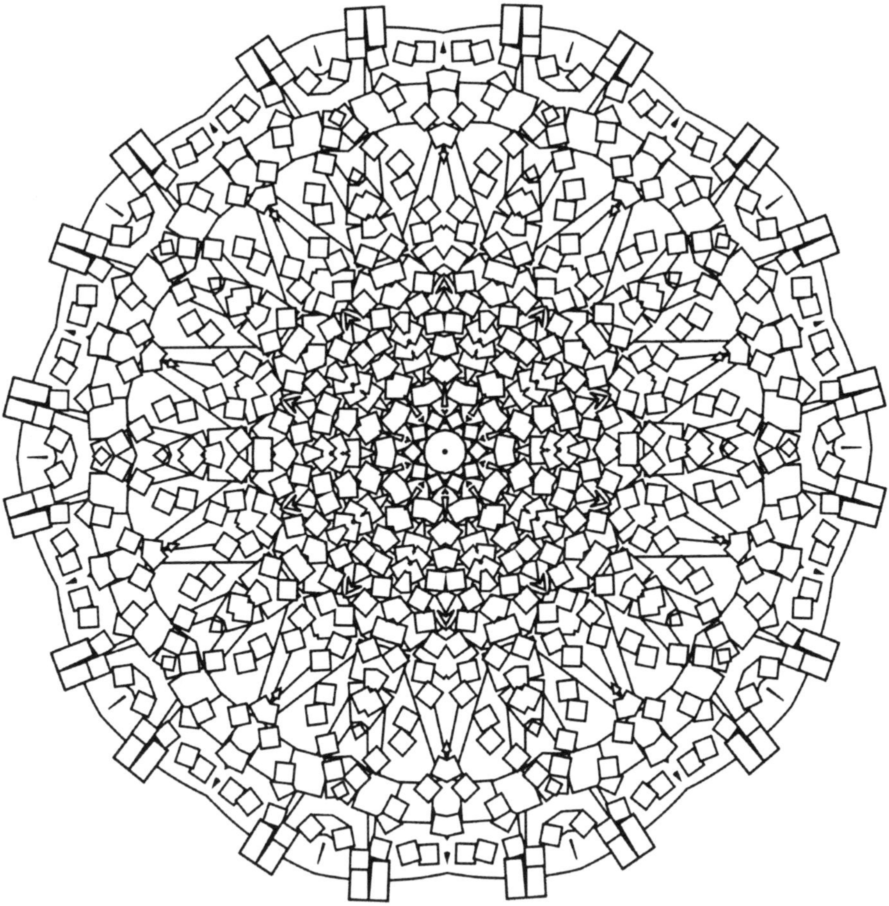

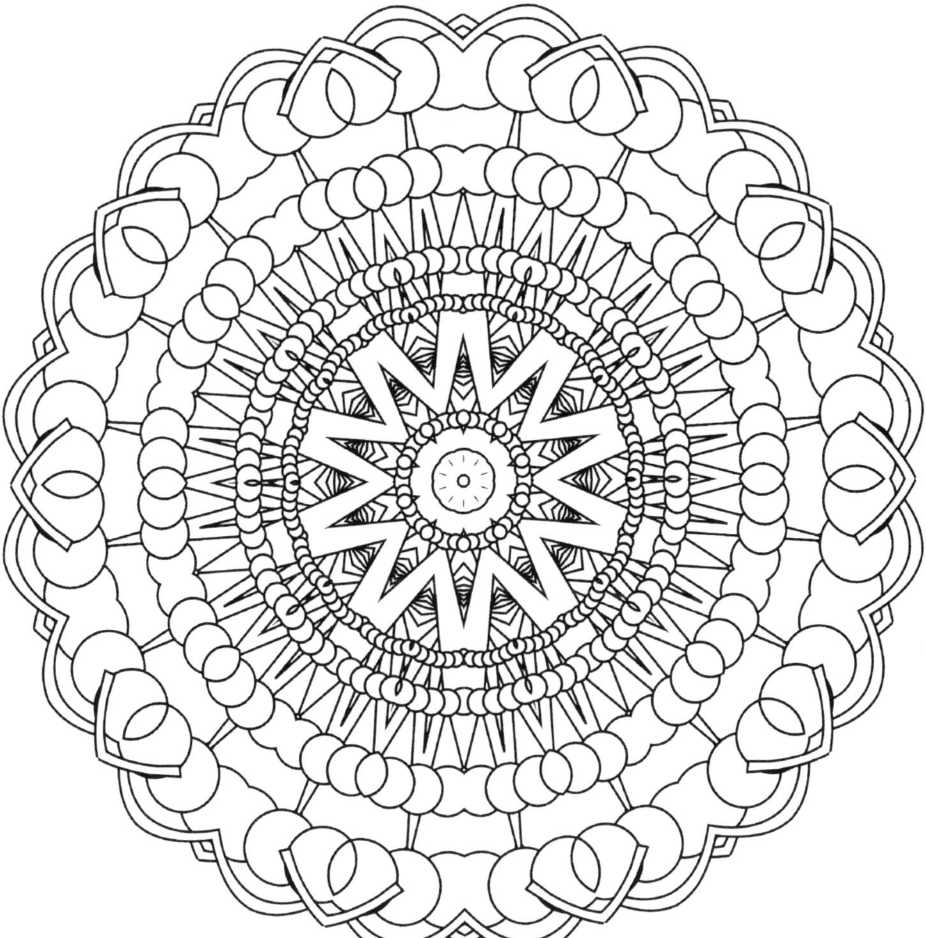

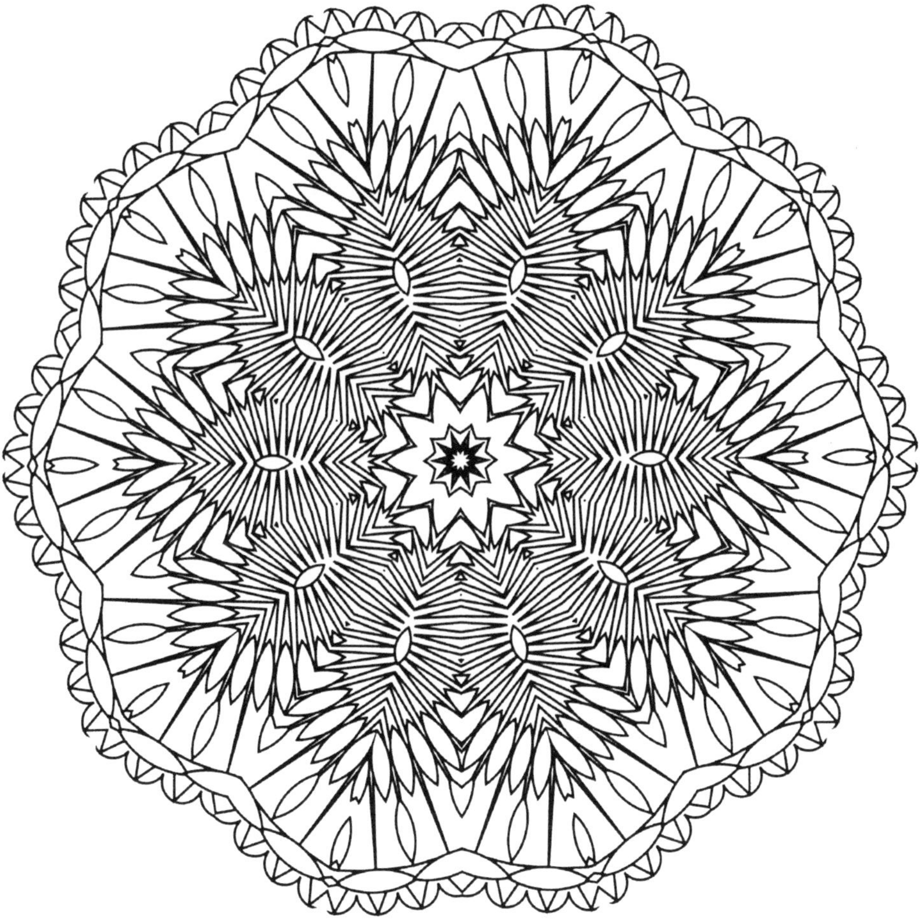

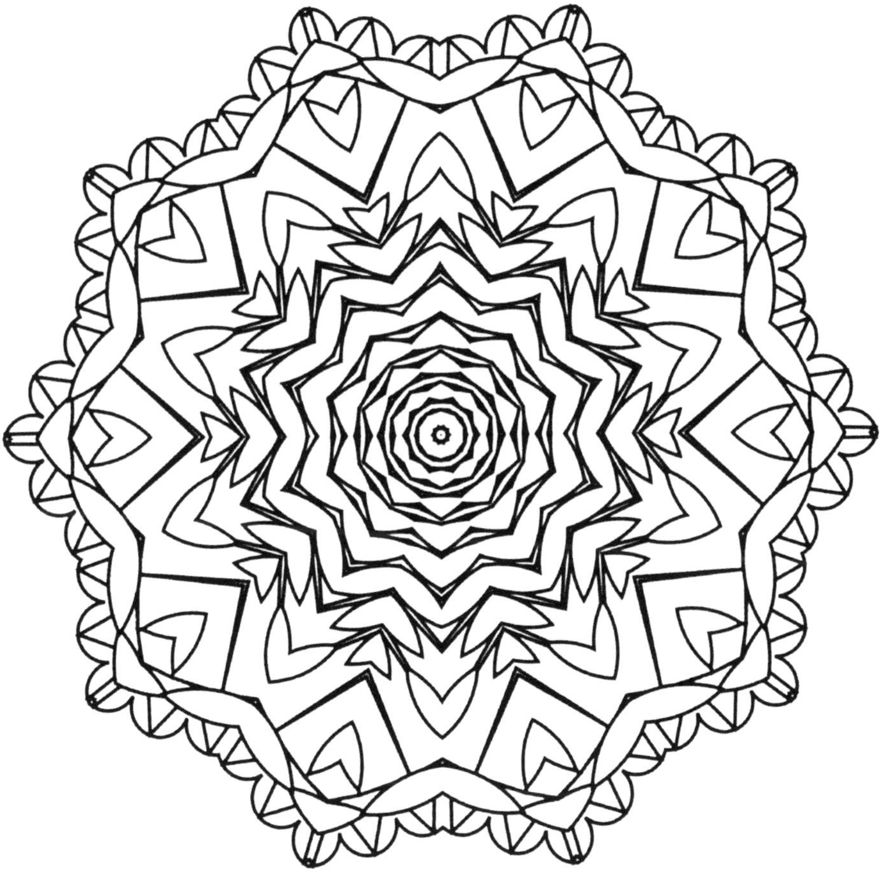

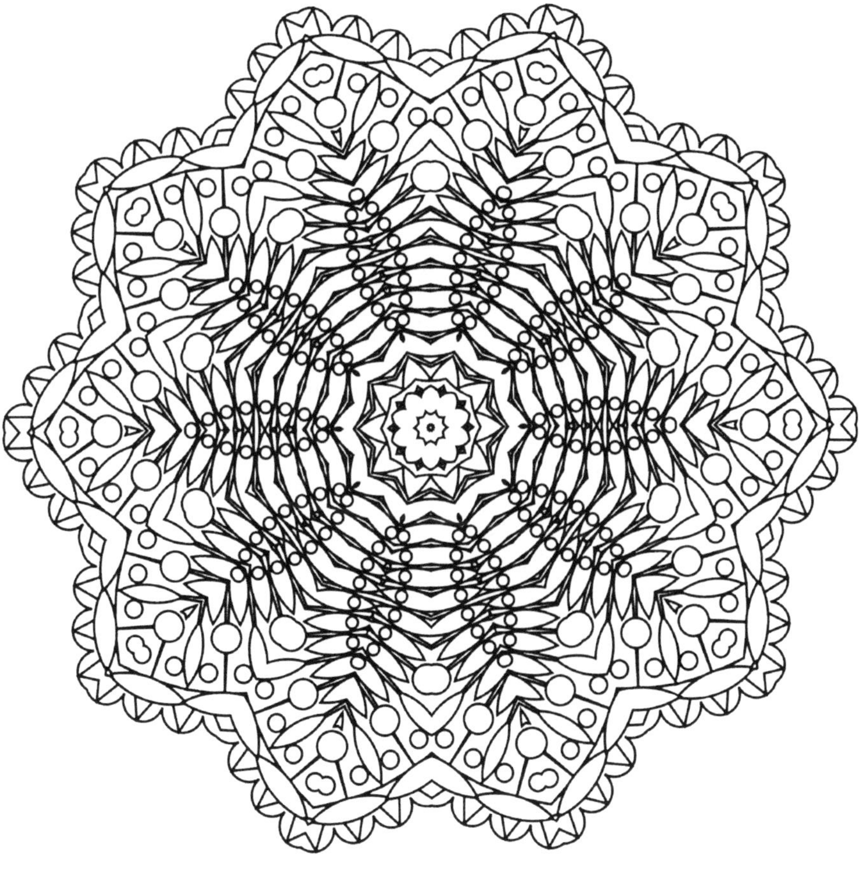

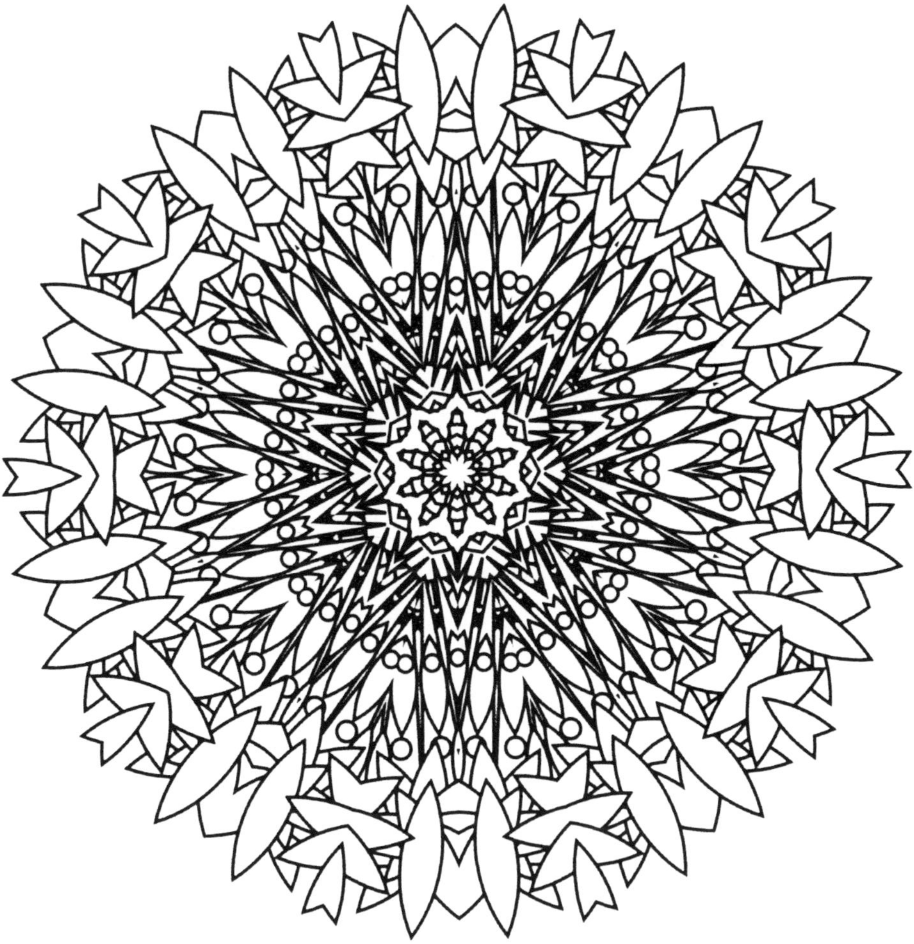

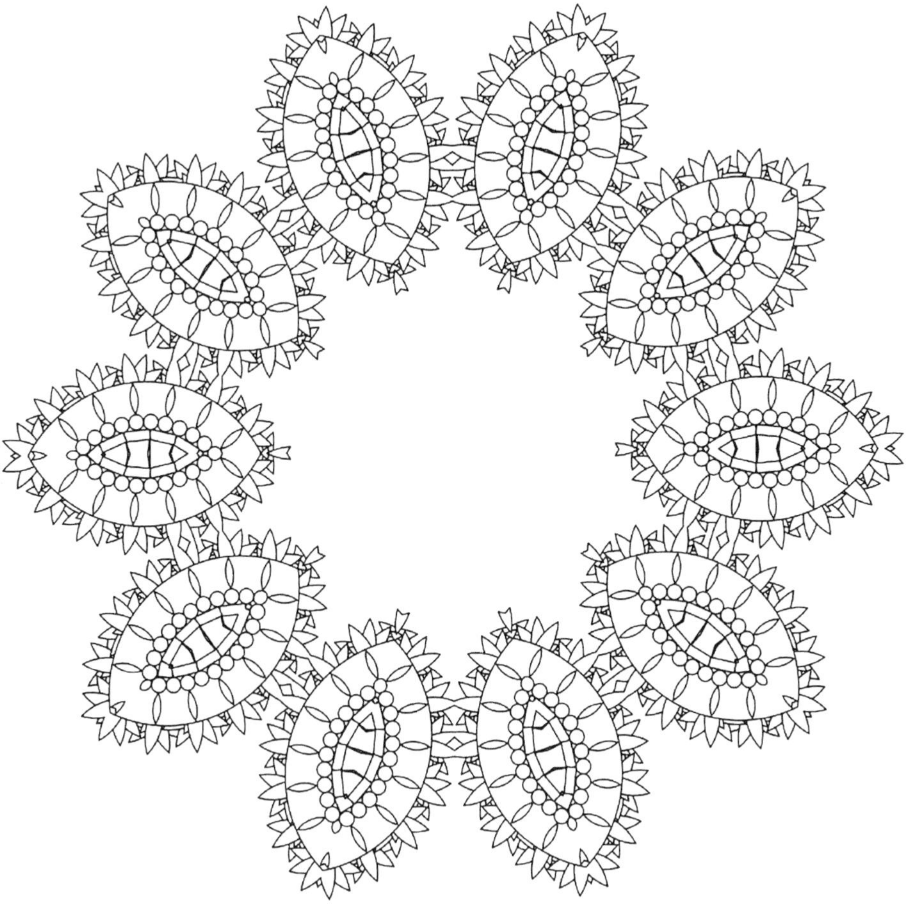

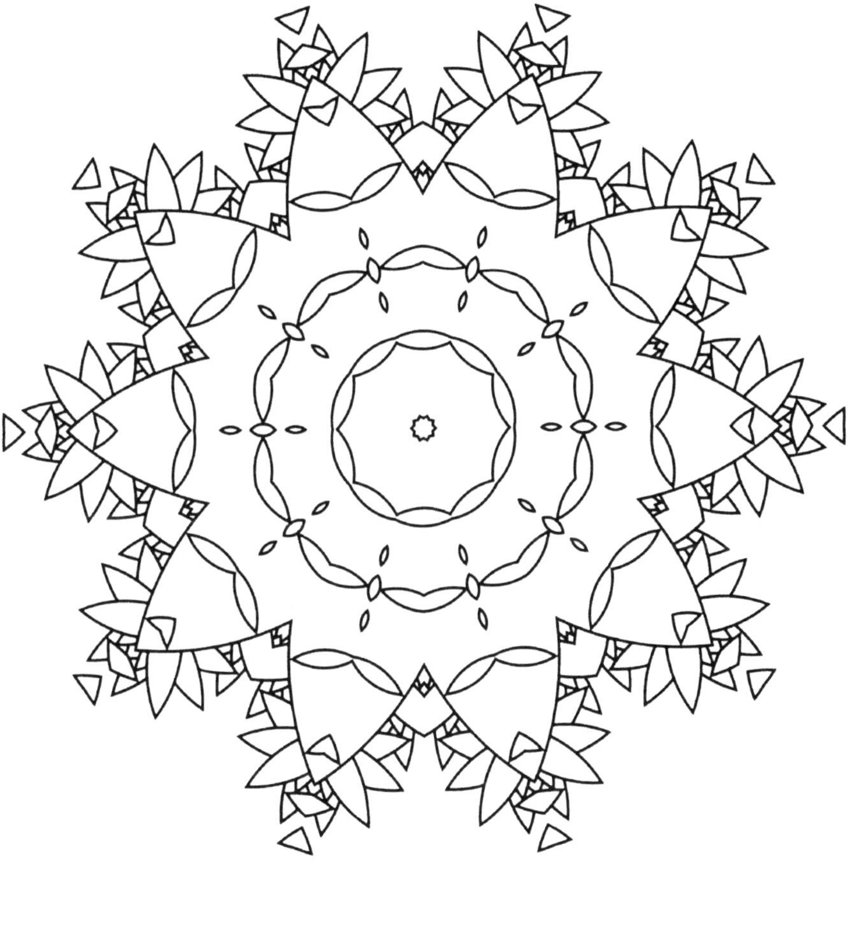

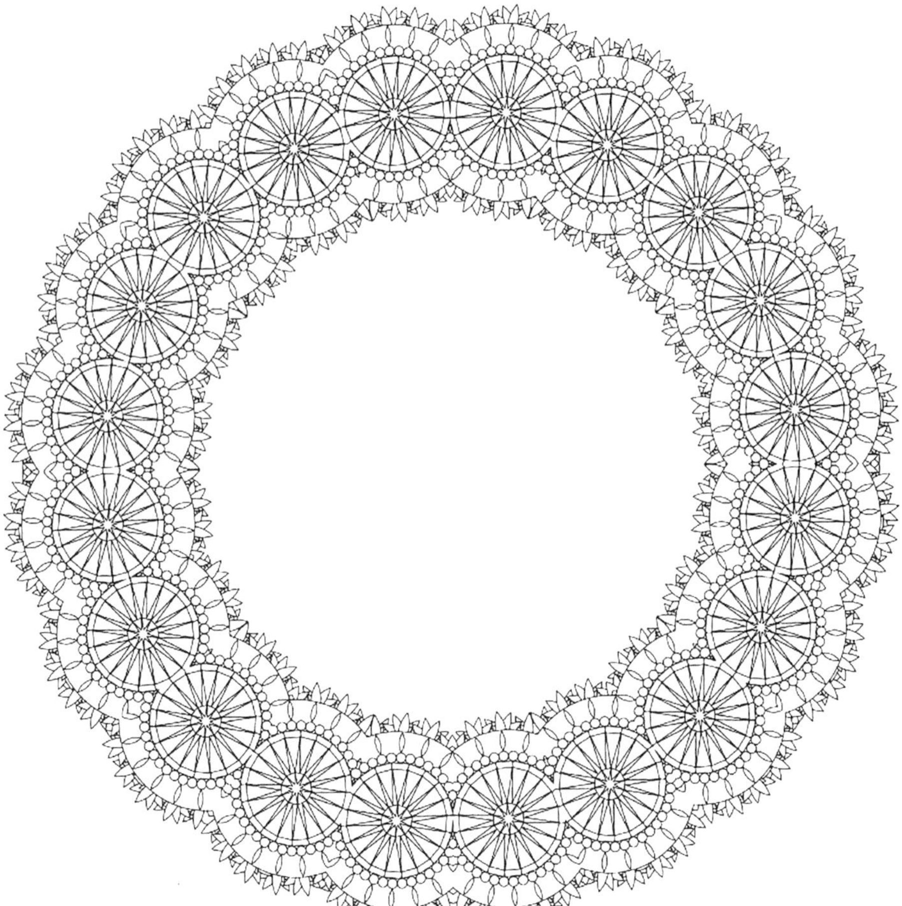

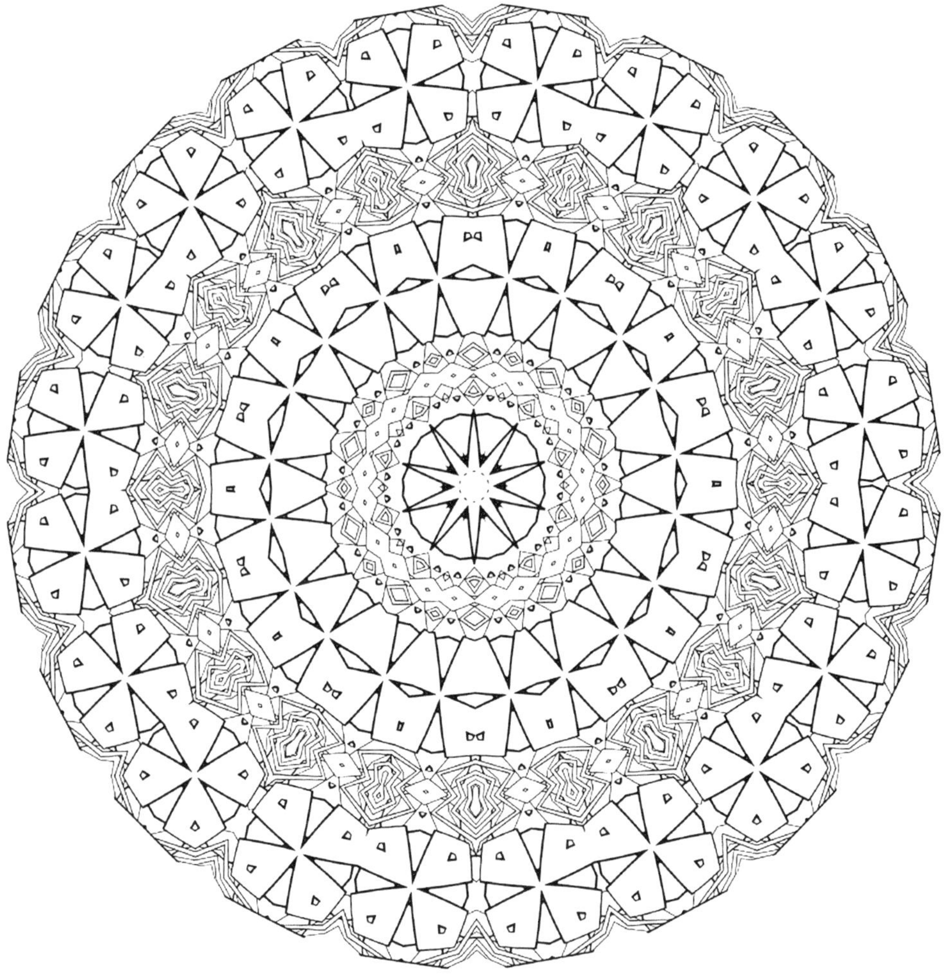

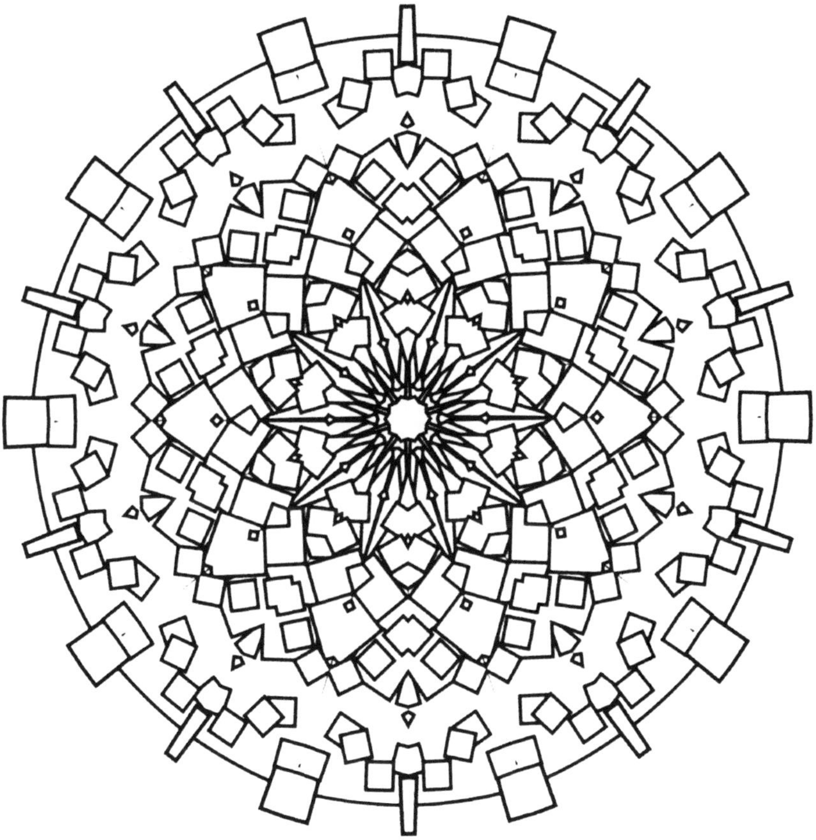

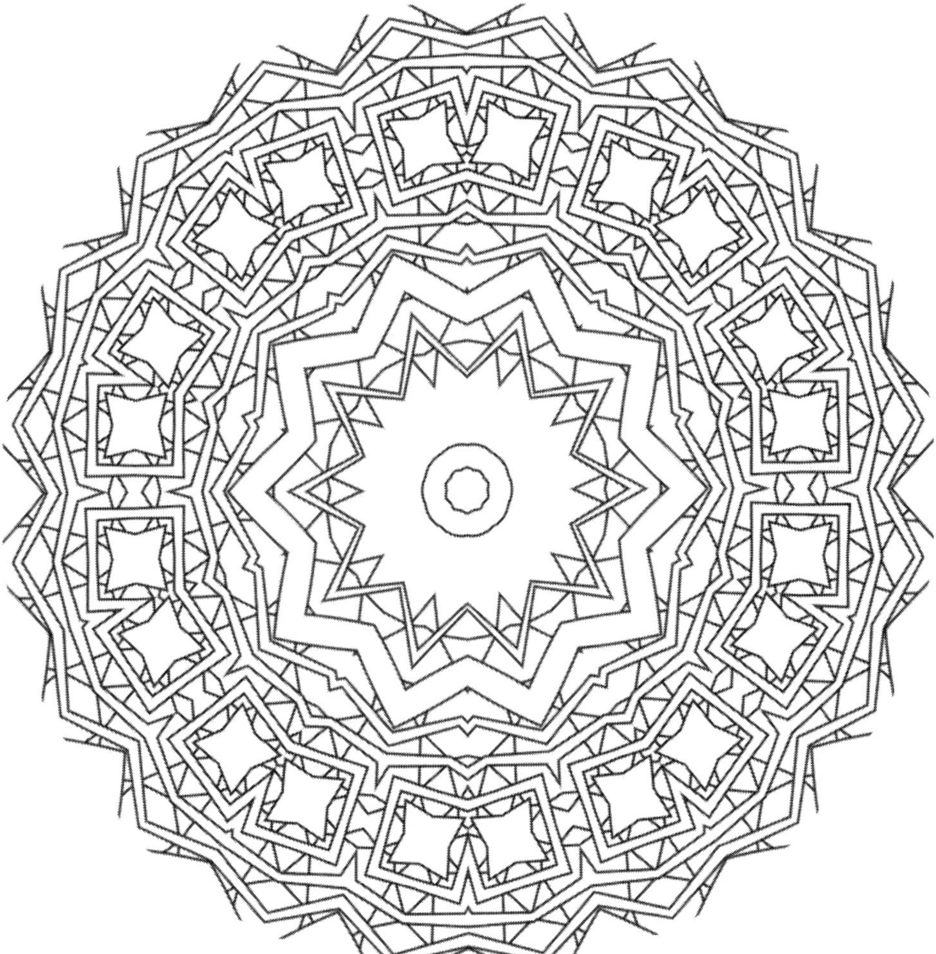

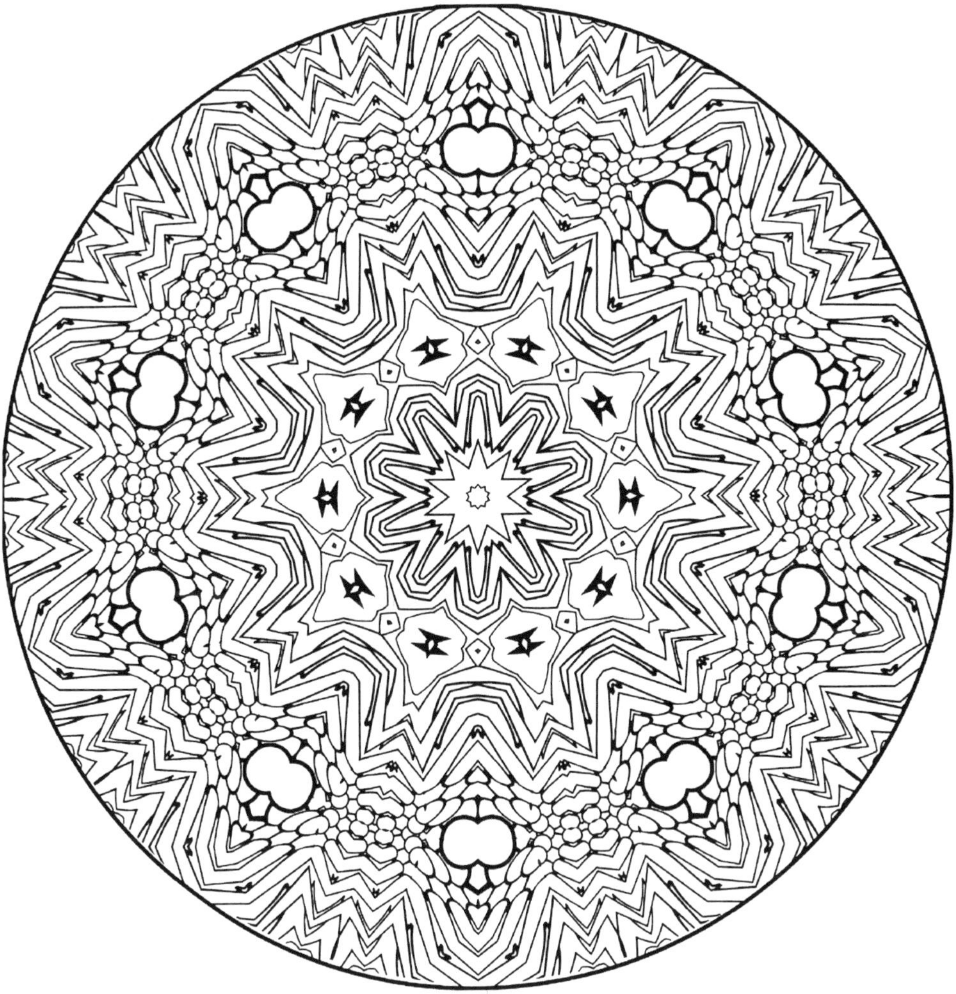

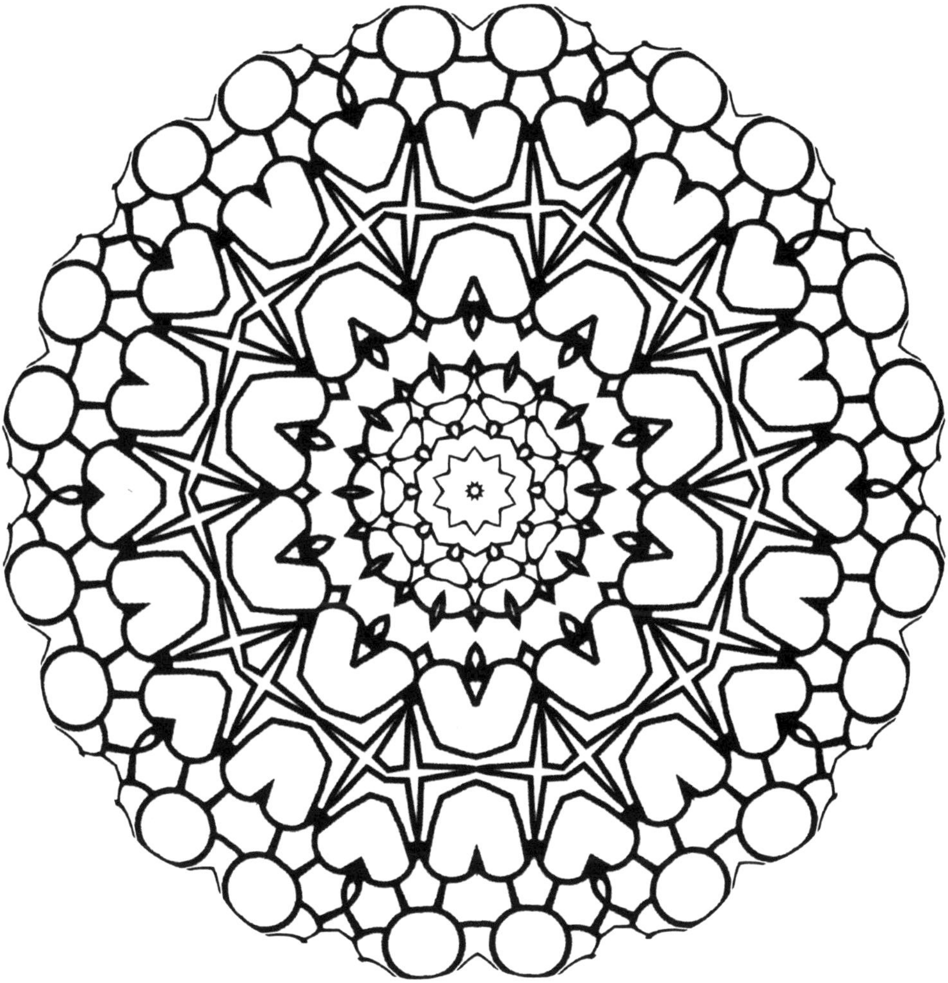

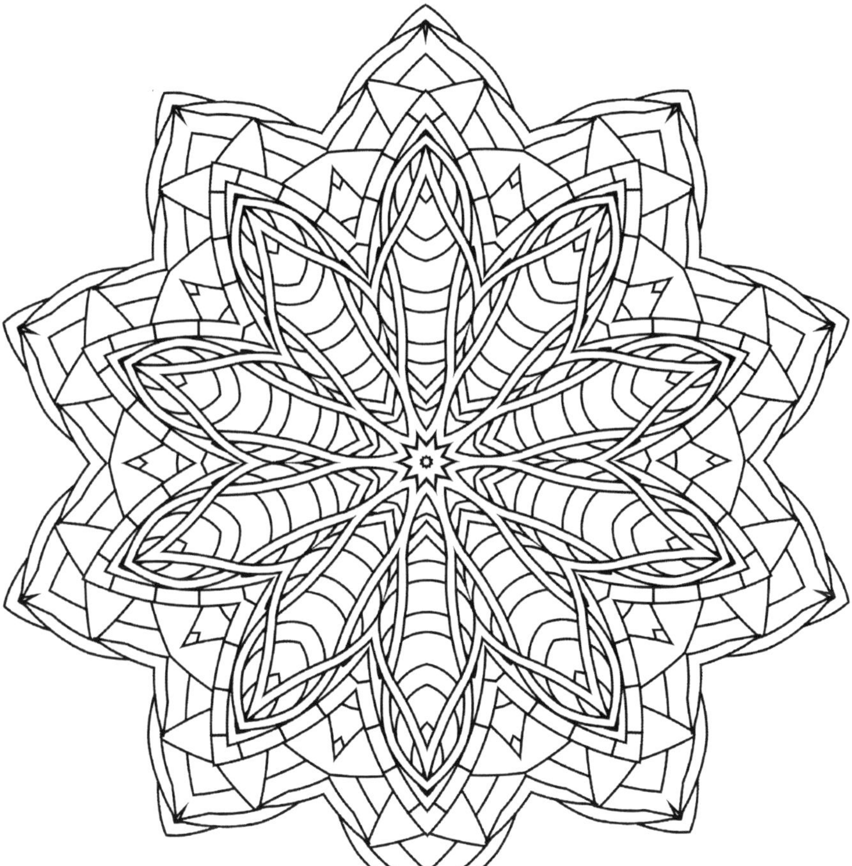

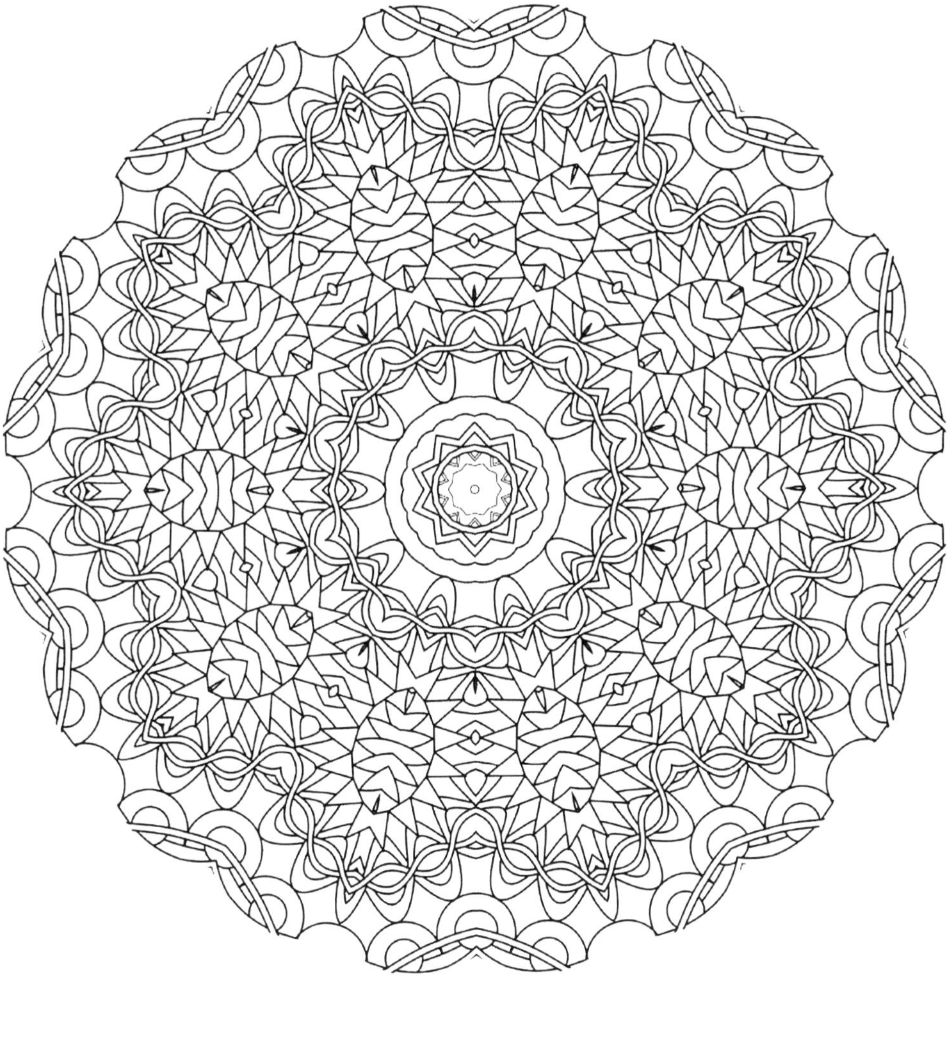

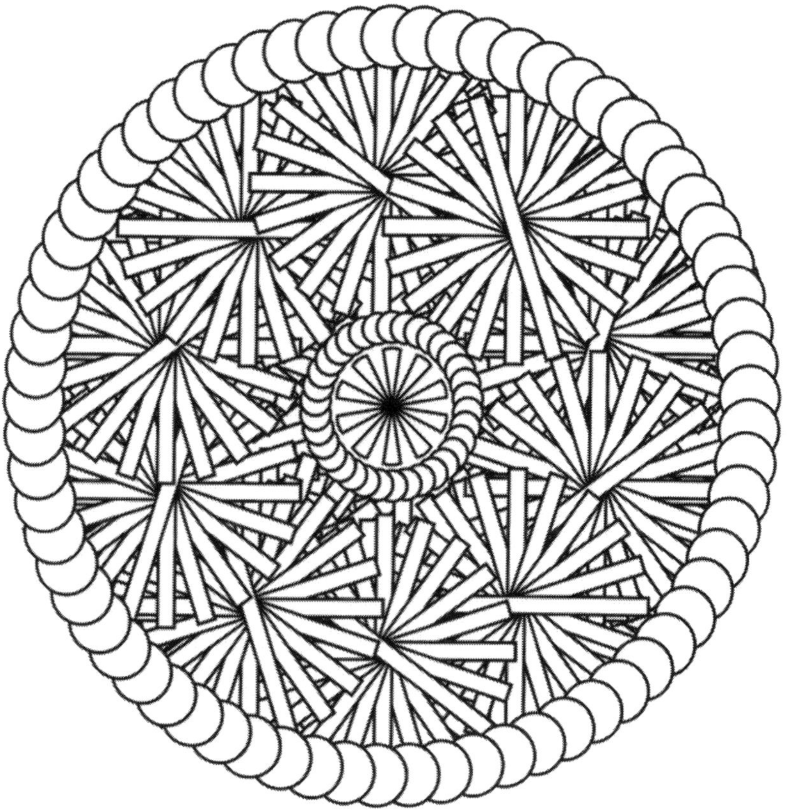

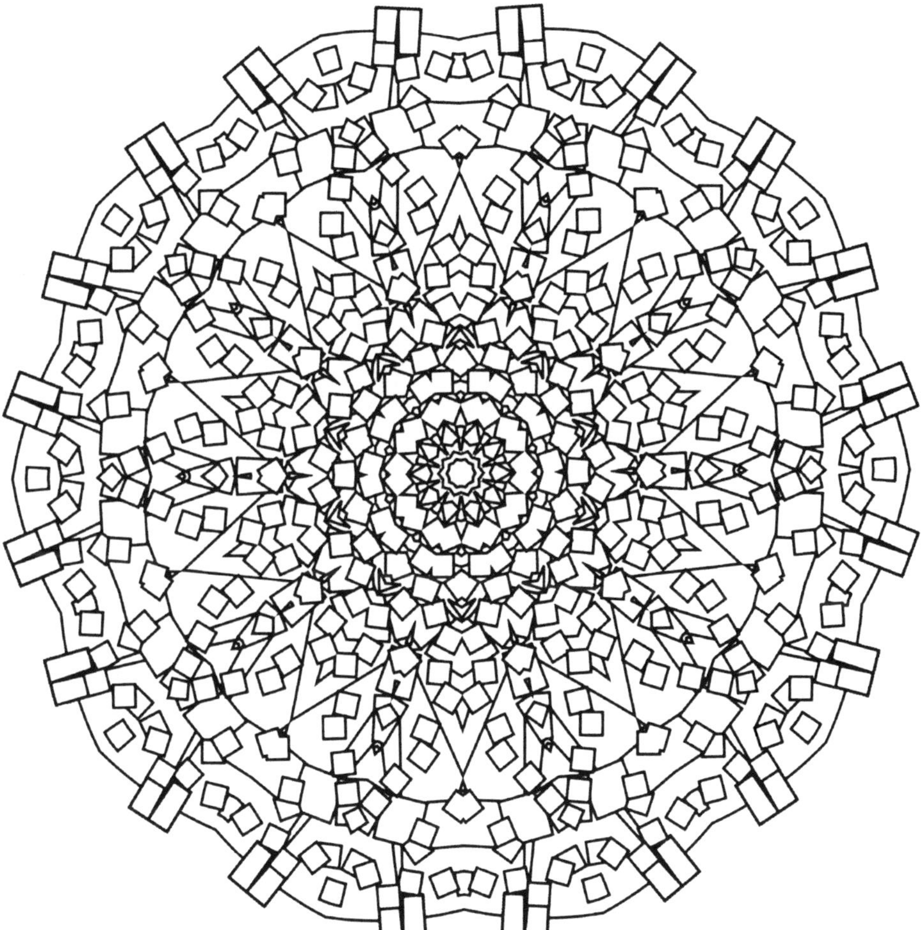

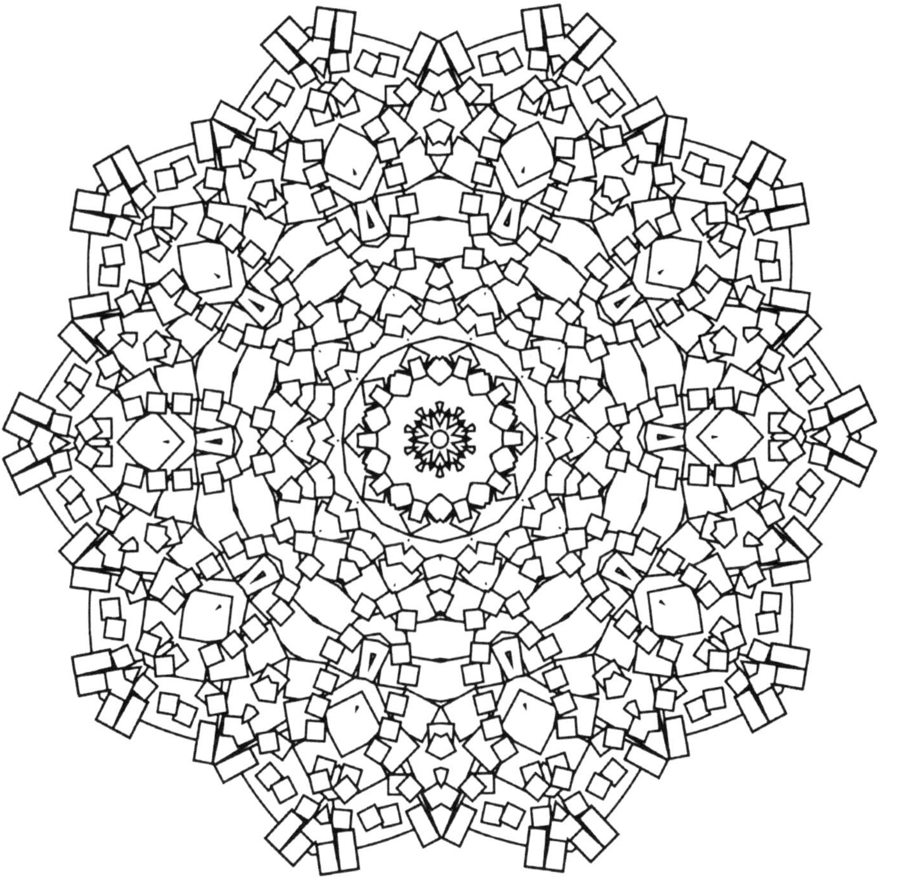

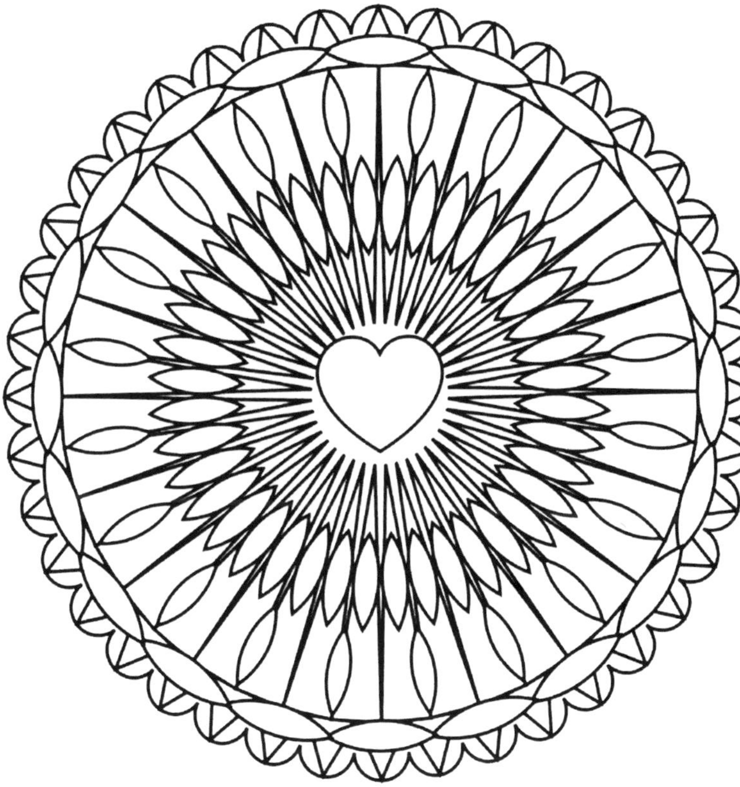

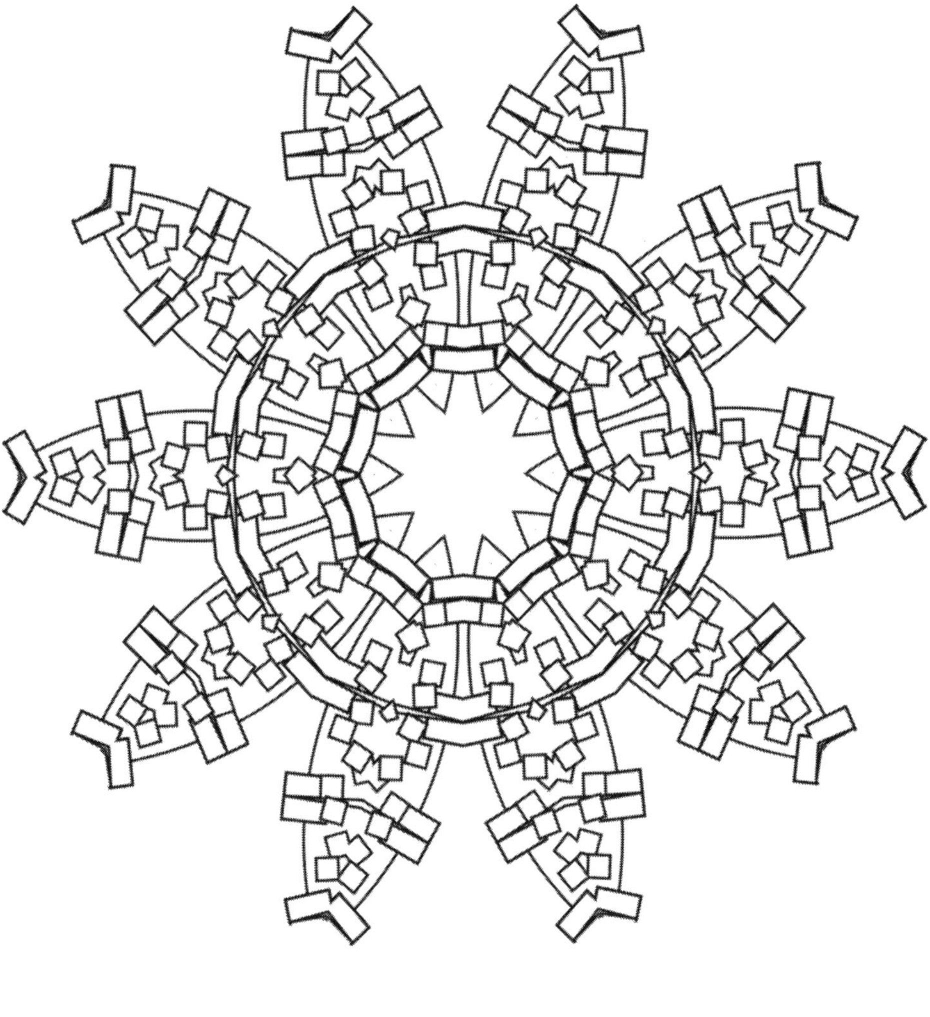

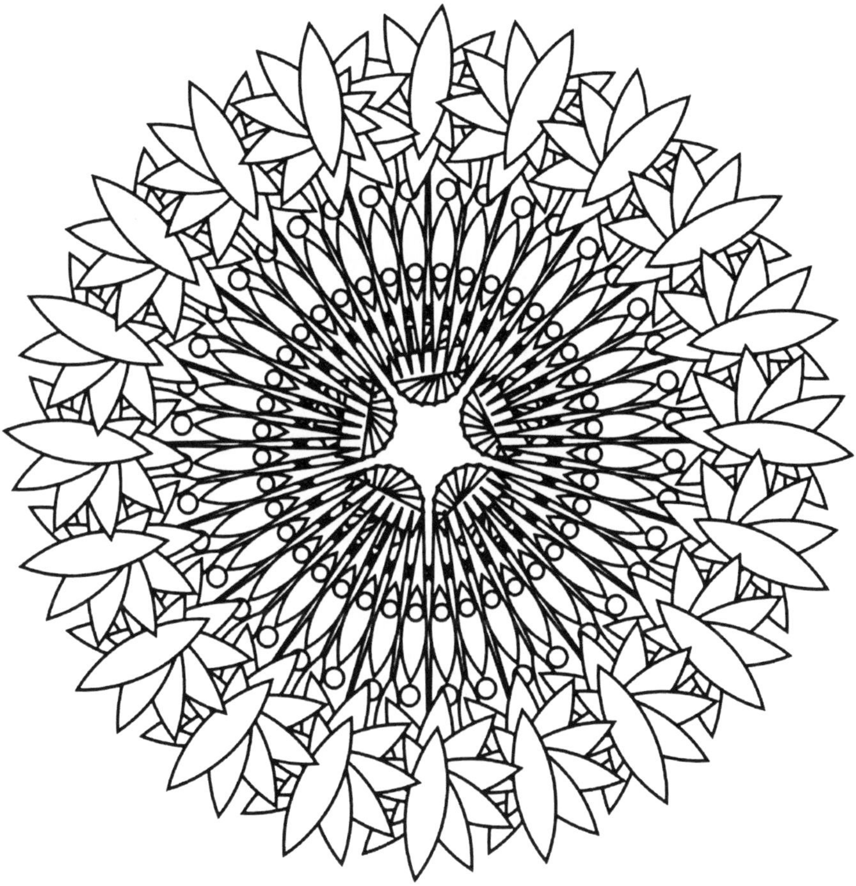

I hope you have enjoyed coloring this book of coloring images.

Perhaps you felt the stresses of the day float away. I hope so.

Check out my other coloring books if you enjoyed this one. There are both mandala and pattern books to choose from.

Keep up to date with adult colouring books from Red Berry Quiz books by joining my list.
You will receive a new adult colour design every two weeks in your inbox. and advance notice of any new books.

To join go to this address:

http://www.redberryquizbooks.com/zllt

Follow me on:

Facebook:
facebook.com/redberrycoloringbooks

Twitter: @quiz_berry

Other Titles available from Red Berry Quiz Books:

Print books:
Inner Peace Volumes 1, 2
Inner Calm volumes 1
Coloring minds Vol 1, 2
Pocket coloring Book

EBooks:
Coloring Minds vol 1
Coloring Minds vol 2

Join the mailing list to receive a free book of coloring images and a coloring image every two weeks
http://www.redberryquizbooks.com/adult-coloring-books-free/

All available from amazon.com, createspace.com and other retailers worldwide.

Printed in Great Britain
by Amazon